T0207671

CAN YOU
Believe It?

15 Key Christian Beliefs about Life that
Will Transform Your Understanding
of God's Purpose for Your Life!

MARK VEE

WESTBOW
P R E S S®
A DIVISION OF THOMAS NELSON
& ZONDERVAN

WestBow Press books may be ordered through booksellers or by contacting:

WestBow Press
A Division of Thomas Nelson & Zondervan
1663 Liberty Drive
Bloomington, IN 47403
www.westbowpress.com
844-714-3454

ISBN: 978-1-6642-1211-4 (sc)
ISBN: 978-1-6642-1212-1 (hc)
ISBN: 978-1-6642-1210-7 (e)

Library of Congress Control Number: 2020922262

Print information available on the last page.

WestBow Press rev. date: 02/15/2021

CONTENTS

DEDICATION

I dedicate this book to my father and mother, Jay and Betty Vredeveld. Two of the greatest influences in my life has been you. My understanding of unconditional love and what it means to become a spiritual blessing, has come from you. Your willingness to hear and care, to do whatever you can to help, has given me the ability to understand what a life of meaning and purpose is.

INTRODUCTION

What do you believe life is all about?

Do you realize what you believe changes your experiences in life?

We are born into this world not having a clue about why we are here or what we are here for. Why is there this planet called earth with people on it, and what are we supposed to be doing here?

Not knowing the answers to these types of questions can make life confusing. Not knowing the purpose of doing anything makes it difficult to know what success even looks like. The fact that our time here is limited in that we all are going to die someday, puts even a greater sense of urgency on discovering what life is all about before it is too late to do anything about it! Why do we exist? What is our purpose for existing? What does it mean to live a successful and meaningful life? What does it take to feel good about who I am and what I am doing here? How do we understand the kinds of things we see happening in this world? Why isn't this life paradise, right here and right now? How do we understand the reasons behind the things that happened to us in our lives?

Since becoming an ordained minister with a Master of Divinity degree from Western Theological Seminary in 1982, and during my nearly forty years of being a Christian minister, I have talked to thousands of people about these types of questions concerning life. What has always amazed me, and given me concern, was the number of people both within and outside of the Christian faith circles who struggle coming up with any clear answer as to what they believe about these mysteries of life. Most of those I have talked to were not quite sure what they believed or what they could trust to be true.

This gives me concern because they are missing out on so many blessings in their lives that simply come from trusting beliefs that are true! I long for them to know and trust some of the things I have learned are true because doing so will give them a much higher quality of life!

I have learned that what we desire and believe in life completely transforms what we experience in life, what happens to us, and what effect we will have on others in our lives. Conversely, I have also learned that putting our faith in beliefs that are not true can be dangerous and potentially devastating to our ability to cope and succeed in life. A simple example would be believing a suspended bridge is safe when it is not. That could be a real letdown! Believing we have no value as a person or any hope for a better future leads some people to suicide! Believing God will buy us a Mercedes Benz and deliver it free to our front door because we call ourselves a Christian can lead to a crisis of faith. Likewise, just believing you cannot do something often results in someone not even trying. What we believe changes what we experience in life!

What I offer here, in a clear and easy-to-understand way, are fifteen key biblical beliefs that unlock the mysteries of life. These beliefs serve as a solid foundation for defining in detail what we call the Christian faith.

I have personally discovered that these biblical beliefs offer the keys to understanding life, ourselves, and other people. It has been my experience that these same beliefs can unleash the presence and spiritual power of God in and through our daily lives.

When I have shared these beliefs with others, many have experienced one of those "ah-ha" moments of a deeper understanding of what is happening and has happened in their lives. I have likewise witnessed people who embrace these beliefs eliminate all kinds of unnecessary fears and experience a higher quality of life that they had never thought possible.

When I was preparing to write this book, I visited my mother to share with her what I was planning. I explained to her that I was going to write a book that would offer a clear and easy to understand account of what the bible teaches us as to what life is all about.

We talked about how so many people today don't have a clue as to what life is all about. They do not know why they are here or what is causing all the problems they face; nor do they have any idea on how to deal with it.

We likewise discussed how different and difficult life is for young people growing up in the world today and about how powerful the influence our beliefs have been in our own experiences in life. After just a short discussion about these things, my mother said, "If you can do that, I will buy twenty-seven of them!"

Parents and grandparents are afraid for young people today who are growing up in this world. What is going to happen to them if they don't have a clear understanding of what life is all about? How are they going to deal with all the different types of stress they are forced to face in their lives today? To what will they turn to when the thrill of a pleasure-seeking life is gone? Most of them will not even hear about these biblical beliefs in that most do not regularly attend churches. How will they cope with the media messages the world is sending as truths about life?

People are being bombarded with massive amounts of information every day that paints a picture of life with no absolute rights and wrongs and where no one is responsible for what they do or what happens in their lives. Collectively, life is often presented as no more than a quest to seek pleasure, be entertained, and look for new ways to satisfy our wants and needs. Is that all life is about?

Now don't take me wrong. I like to experience pleasure and like to avoid pain as much as the next person. Doing so at times is a good thing, but it is not the purpose of life. People who live their lives just to be entertained will end up living a life of quiet desperation to just survive. People who have no more to live for than that will struggle to maintain any healthy sense of self-worth.

Living a good life that is fulfilling and satisfying—that makes a positive difference in the lives of other people—cannot be found in simply seeking pleasure and avoiding pain. Clearly defining our beliefs about life is a crucial step to living a successful and rewarding life in the world we experience today!

What will these fifteen beliefs do for you?

Through embracing these biblical beliefs with faith, you will experience the confidence that comes from having a clear biblical understanding of what life is all about. Your sense of self-esteem and self-worth will steadily rise as you live with a clear sense of purpose and direction for your life.

Embracing these key foundational beliefs of the Christian faith into your understandings about life will enable you to experience being freed from many of the fears that permeate our societies today. Your faith will be strengthened and your hope renewed. You will be equipped to daily focus on what is important in life and will be given spiritual eyes to see and ears to hear what the perfect will of God is.

These beliefs are what apostle Paul was talking about when he told believers to be transformed by the renewing of your mind.

> Do not conform to the pattern of this world but be transformed by the *renewing* of your mind. Then you will be able to test and approve what God's will is—his good, pleasing, and perfect will. (Romans 12:2)

Your life will be transformed as you incorporate these beliefs into your thinking and goals in life.

Can You Believe It?

I understand these are bold claims for what one book can do, but my experience has shown me that those that can embrace these beliefs as true will have a clearer understanding of the purpose of their lives and they will increasingly experience the spiritual power of God being unleashed in and through their lives.

ONE

Is There Anybody Out There?

FAITH KEY #1

GOD THE CREATOR EXISTS AND IS HERE!

In the beginning, God created the heavens and the earth. (Genesis 1:1 NIV)

In Grand Haven, Michigan, where I live, is a tall hill known as Five Mile Hill. The reason they call it that is because before there was a lighthouse in Grand Haven someone had to go to the top of that hill with a lantern to guide ships into the harbor. Five miles was how far away people on a ship could see the light of a lantern being held up on the top of this hill.

From the top of Five Mile Hill is an incredible panoramic view of Grand Haven and the surrounding area. One day when I was at the top of this hill, I looked out to the west and began enjoying the beauty of Lake Michigan. I could see the sparkling-blue waters of the lake stretch down to the horizon and out to the west. People come and see beautiful sunsets with a vast variety of breathtaking colors.

As I was enjoying this colorful display of beauty, I looked over to the right, and I saw the channel where the Grand River deposits into Lake Michigan. On either side of the river, I saw the two piers of Grand

1

Haven. The south pier uniquely stands out with the very recognizable two red lighthouses and catwalk that runs to the end of the pier.

As I gazed at the beauty of the two Grand Haven Piers, it came to my mind that those piers exist for more reasons than just for their beauty. Those piers were not always there. Somebody came up with the idea for a pier, and they had a reason for building them. There are functional reasons why they exist, where they exist, and subsequently how they were built. These piers were created with purpose and meaning.

Someone also created the big lighthouse at the end of the south pier for a reason. That pier and lighthouse would not exist if there were not reasons and a purpose behind their existence.

You can also look to the east and north from Five Mile Hill and see the city of Grand Haven below. There, you can overlook the streets and houses, neatly stacked in rows, and farther off to the left, you can see the stores located in downtown Grand Haven.

And again, it came to my mind that all these things exist for a purpose and a reason. These things would not exist if it were not for that purpose and reason. That these things exist at all is evidence that there was someone with a purpose and reason behind their creation.

I could also see people and cars going down the road, and I wondered why they were there. There must be a reason—some purpose for them being there.

Likewise, I could see all kinds of plants and trees of various shapes and sizes. As I took it all in, I saw that it was all quite beautiful. But I have also learned that there is more to their existence than just beauty's sake. There is a reason for their existence. They have purpose and meaning for their existence that gives them a value beyond what just meets the eye.

The plants and trees are taking carbon monoxide out of the air and producing the oxygen we need to live and breathe. There are valuable reasons for their existence, and subsequently that is evidence that someone created them.

I exist. You exist. These facts give evidence that someone created us for a reason. Like everything else in creation, there is purpose and reasons behind our existence.

The number one belief of biblical Christian faith is that God exists and is the Creator of all things. He is a living spiritual presence among us who not only created things the way they are, but His presence and power are also what holds things in the order and the interactive states in which we find them.

The belief that God the Creator exists is the number one foundational element of Christian faith. God is the intelligence, the reason, and the creating power behind everything that exists. Life and each thing in creation have meaning and purpose because God created everything for a reason. Both you and I have value, meaning, and purpose because God has wonderfully created us for His purposes.

The concept of the existence of one God who created everything is a belief that all Christians trust to be true. If this Christian belief is true, we have come to know it is true only because God has revealed Himself to us. If this belief is not true, no religious or theological teaching has any significant meaning or value.

My belief in the existence of God, however, is not just a blind leap of faith or a random choice of beliefs. I believe God has provided us with an enormous amount of evidence that He exists, even though I do not understand everything about Him. The concept of a creator is what makes rational sense based on the things I do know from my own experiences to be true.

The self-revelation of the existence of God to me has been like the effect of wind in the air. I cannot see the wind, but I see the effects of the wind. When the presence of the wind is strong, I feel it. I can see it in the trees and the rustling of leaves around me. Even though I cannot see the wind, I can feel it on my face, and I know it is there. We can experience unseen things. When the wind is calm, I do not notice it, and someone who has never experienced its presence could even argue that it does not exist. Sometimes in my life, the presence of God has been extraordinarily strong, and at other times, the only evidence of the presence of God was my faith.

The existence of God in creation is shown using the concept of cause and effect. Every action creates a reaction. Like every step leaves a footprint, I see God's footprints all over His creation. The intricacy of nature, of science, of all interactive systems in our world, and even the interactive complexities of our human bodies, is evidence of intelligence beyond this world.

The example of the miracle of birth, when a unique spiritual being enters this world through the womb, is evidence of something more than a mere biological event. A spiritual being, who can reason and communicate, has entered the world through the miracle of birth.

Someone made things the way they are, the way they work, and the way they interact with each other. That intelligence, that someone, that designer, that energy that runs the universe, is God our Creator.

Let me explain further with an example of a painter. When I see a painting, I see something that someone has created, not something that has always existed. I see evidence of a level of intelligence and reason in the painting. I see that the creator of the painting made choices of what to show in the painting, what colors to use, the shade of light, and so on. Just like a painting, the whole creation is evidence of the existence and glory of God. The whole creation declares the existence and glory of God (Job 12:7, 10; Psalm 19:1, 4; Romans 1:20).

Similarly, when I add two plus two and get four, I see additional evidence of intelligence, an order of things that is true, and an order of things that is maintained. Why does two plus two equal four? It is because that is the way God made it. It adds up. It makes sense. It has a functional purpose and meaning. It is evidence of the existence and nature of an intelligent God. A far greater stretch is to believe that everything exists as it does because of an explosion that just happened to leave things as they are.

I believe God exists, and I also believe He wants us to know He exists and is more than willing and able to reveal Himself to anyone open to this truth. When I say that I have faith in God, I am saying I trust my belief that God the Creator exists is an objective truth—it is a reality. There is purpose and reason behind our existence.

Some in the scientific community believe and teach that when the scientific, empirical evidence is studied, we can trace our existence back to what they have named the big bang. They say that a long time ago—several billion years ago—there was a big bang, an explosion that created the entire universe as we know it. They do not know exactly why it happened, or what existed before the big bang, but when it happened, everything that exists was created.

Now I believe that is a fine theory, and I feel no need to argue the point on their terms. If it is true, I believe what existed before the bang and the reason for the bang was God! God is the cause and reason behind everything that exists (Hebrews 11:3).

Genesis 1:1 says, "In the beginning, God created the heavens and the earth." I do not doubt there was a big bang too when God said, "Let there be light," and suddenly there was light (Genesis 1:3)!

I believe a scientific discovery will never be a real threat to the belief in God as the Creator. Science is only examining the footprints of God. Every detail discovered through scientific inquiries is only learning how God created things and maintains things as they are. Each accurate scientific discovery only adds to the wonder, power, and glory of our Creator.

I dare you—no, I double dare you—to dream up any scenario about the origin of our existence, and I guarantee you will still have to conclude one of two things: (1) the why or reason behind your theory will have to be the concept of God or (2) there is no why or reason behind our existence. If you decide to believe there is no reason behind our existence, then nothing matters anyway. If you decide there is a Creator, everything that exists is a testament to the power and intelligence of our Creator.

The existence of God is what gives life purpose and meaning. God created the heavens and the earth for a reason. There are purposes and reasons behind everything God created. God created mankind and gave us life for a reason.

That you and I are here makes us precious because like everything else, there is a reason someone has created us. Contrarily, a world without God would have no purpose or meaning at all.

What makes sense to you? Do you believe there is a God? Do you believe there is an intelligent creator behind all that exists?

I believe it is important that you consider this question yourself and decide for yourself, what do you believe? What makes sense to you? Do you believe there is a God? Do you believe there is an intelligence with power that created everything that exists for a reason?

I believe in God the Father Almighty, maker of heaven and earth. Do you? Why?

> By faith, we understand that the universe was formed at God's command so that what is seen was not made out of what was visible. (Hebrews 11:3)
>
> And without faith, it is impossible to please him, for whoever would draw near to God must believe that he exists and that he rewards those who seek him. (Hebrews 11:6)

To fully realize and experience the comforting spiritual blessing of this truth requires more than just saying, "I believe God exists." This truth must be internalized and incorporated into our thinking and understanding of our existence. We experience the benefits of this truth when this belief becomes the foundation of our faith, and we daily trust God, the Creator and the designer of all things that exist, and who is still with us here and now.

When I am confronted at times by the fact that many things that can affect my life are out of my control, I begin dealing with it by consciously trusting this belief that we are not alone in this world.

When I meditate on how God our Creator understands everything, has the power to do anything, and is in control of everything, I enjoy the spiritual blessings of the peace and comfort that comes from knowing all creation is not out of control. It gives me confidence that we are not helplessly vulnerable to random catastrophes. A creator is in control of all things that have been created. I believe the Creator spoken of in scripture exists, and I intentionally trust daily that to be true in my heart and mind.

In creation, we discover God designed us with needs that must be met for us to live. We also discover, in the creation, how those needs are being met by God as well. I do not believe the things needed to sustain life on this planet are a fortunate coincidence of chance. I believe that our needs and how these needs are being met are part of the intentional design of our Creator. The presence and power of God Almighty holds everything together as it exists. God designed, created, and maintains the environment needed to support life.

I believe in God the Father Almighty, maker of heaven and earth. Do you?

I believe God will reveal himself to all who desire to know the Truth, and the truth of His existence will set you free from the fears that exist if He didn't (Jeremiah 29:13).

Each of us must decide for ourselves. What do you believe and why?

TWO

How Can You Trust a God Like That?

FAITH KEY #2

GOD IS GOOD.

For the Lord is good and his love endures forever; his faithfulness continues through all generations. (Psalm 100:5 NIV)

Since I believe God exists and is continually present with us in this world, I walked outside unto my deck early one morning and decided I wanted to experience the healing presence of God right then and there. I wanted God to strengthen my faith in Him by speaking to me right then and there, and throughout the rest of the day.

I was looking for God to continue to heal the spiritual wounds and scars left in my heart that were inflicted by my sins and the sins of others. I was looking for God to heal and purify my heart, so I would be able to love Him and others as a spiritual child of God.

I was looking to God with faith to free me from the lies and the subsequent fears that God's love for me is not unconditional. I was looking to be freed from doubting that God can be trusted to meet all my physical and spiritual needs and to be freed from the fear that my sins could separate me from the daily and eternal blessings of God.

I was looking for God to speak to me and thereby equip me to live in the light, even as Jesus lived in the light. I was looking for God to show me and tell me what I could do and say to love others and help usher in the spiritual kingdom of God through my life. So, I waited on God.

It was early morning, and as I was waiting on God, my mind was soon drawn to the darkness that surrounded me. The thought occurred to me how fortunate we are to live in a world with light.

I imagined all the ways life would be diminished if we had to live in a world without light. Sure, it is something everyone takes for granted, but it is a huge blessing for everyone and everything living on this planet. To live a life in darkness would be a life filled with continual uncertainty and fear. I thought, how fortunate we are to find ourselves on a planet with light!

As the light increased around me, I felt the growing warmth of the sun on my face, and it gave me a sense of comfort and peace that all was right in my world. Again, a thought occurred to me how fortunate we are to have the warmth that comes from the sun. Our bodies are designed to sustain life only within a small range of temperatures. Without that warmth, we would all die. How fortunate we are to find ourselves on a planet that sustains a temperature that supports life!

As I enjoyed the experience of the growing beauty of the morning in that light and the warmth of the sun, I became conscious of my breathing. I took a deep breath and again a thought occurred to me that without that oxygen we couldn't even live! How fortunate we are to find ourselves on a planet that produces oxygen needed for us to even live! And likewise, how even more incredible that we have a body with lungs that are designed to process that air needed for us to live!

At this point, I noticed the trees and bushes that were around me, and another thought came to me. We even have trees and bushes that filter out the poisonous carbon monoxide we exhale and produce more oxygen to sustain our life! Again, the thought, how fortunate!

I then thought to wonder, "Why?" The scientific answer is that we have the light and warmth necessary to support life on this planet because of the sun. That answer is not, however, why, but how? Science discovers answers about how things work but not why.

The answer of Christian faith to why is God! I believe in God, the Father Almighty—the maker of heaven and earth. God created everything that exists, and we are designed as the crowning focus of His creation. God created us and designed us with needs that must be met for us to live. God likewise accordingly created and sustains everything needed to meet our physical and spiritual needs for life. The truth about God and His love for us is all around us!

In each passing moment, as these thoughts kept coming to my mind, the sense of the presence of God, and His love for me kept growing.

The thought occurred to me that God did not create this world like a windup clock that He left here and that just keeps running while He went away somewhere else. I was experiencing the active presence of God and His love for me in the revealing light that surrounded me, in the warmth of the air, and with every life-giving breath, I took. God and His love are not just concepts; He is a living presence, and His love for us is a truth we do experience daily, though often unaware.

On hundreds of occasions like that morning on my deck, while looking to God to heal my spiritual brokenness, free me from my spiritual blindness, and speak to me about life, I have experienced the reality of the presence of our loving God.

By seeking God in faith, I experience that God is more than willing and able to reveal Himself to us. By seeking God in faith, I experience the truth that God is good, loves us all unconditionally, and spiritually rewards those who seek Him (Hebrews 11:6).

When people say that they believe in God, their concept of God makes a significant difference in how they understand life and how they live their lives. What do you think God is like?

Consider someone who believes that God demands that people bow down before Him, and if they don't, they will suffer severe consequences, and that God is someone who makes commands, and if you break any of His commandments, He is just waiting to punish you with the pain of everlasting fire!

What kind of effect does that have on how you feel about Him? How would that concept of God affect your desire to trust Him? What effect does faith in a God like that have on people's lives?

Consider someone who believes God will not answer your prayers, nor will He help you unless you are obedient to Him. What effect will it have on your faith in God if you believe you must earn His love and blessings?

Alternatively, consider someone who believes God loves you unconditionally and loves you regardless of whether you have been good or bad. (John 3:16) Consider a God who longs to help and bless you even though you are living far from a perfect life.

Consider a God who understands and sympathizes with people who are confused and struggling to be good people. Consider a God who weeps with those who weep and rejoices with those who rejoice. Consider a God who will do everything He can to give you the gift of eternal life and will help you become the best person you can be, here and now (1 Timothy 2:4).

Consider a God who will forgive your sins and purify you from all unrighteousness (1 John 1:9). Consider a God who will help you become in every way a lovable person who is likewise a continual blessing to other people.

Can you see from these contrasting views how your concept of God and your beliefs about God will make a difference in how you feel about God and what it means when you say, "I believe in God?" Can you see how your concept of God affects your sense of hope, your inner sense of peace, and your hopeful expectations for your future?

To experience the spiritual blessings of God, it is crucial to develop an accurate understanding of God.

When I hear some people describe who they think God is, I often conclude that I too would not love and trust in a God like that either! I too would run and hide from a God who is looking to punish me for something I have said and done wrong!

There is no way we can address a detailed concept of the nature of God here in one chapter. Hundreds of things we believe about God will dramatically affect our experiences of life and our sense of hope, peace, and love in life.

However, what we believe to be true about God will be the foundation for all the other beliefs we have about life and death. Our beliefs about God are part of the foundation that enables us to trust Him with our lives and trust in Him when facing our own deaths. Our beliefs about God affect our hopes and concerns for those we love. These beliefs likewise will affect our thoughts and actions toward one another.

At the heart of the ministry of Jesus Christ was the correction of misconceptions about the character and will of God and the revelation of the true nature of God to us. Jesus is biblically presented as the human incarnation of God who revealed the true nature of God and His love for us.

The ultimate demonstration of the unconditional love of God was seen in the willingness of Jesus to die on a cross to offer us salvation, the forgiveness of sin, a new spiritual relationship with God, and the eternal gift of life in the Holy Spirit.

If you at this point don't believe Jesus was the world's Messiah—the human incarnation of God that brought salvation for everyone in the world—that's okay. That too requires a revelation of Truth from God, and I trust He is more than willing and able to reveal the Truth to you.

The prayer I prayed before experiencing the reality of God's unconditional love and salvation through Jesus Christ was asking God to not let me get sucked into believing some made-up religious story. I wanted to believe in Jesus Christ only if He was truly the Son of God and God-given savior of the world. Thank God, He did.

I believe God revealed to me the Good News of Jesus Christ is true. Since I started trusting that this belief is true, I experience the sense of peace that comes from the forgiveness of sin. I experience a very vivid sense of the presence of God in my life.

I received the gift of the Holy Spirit, and He has been revealing Truth and showing me the way to live ever since. I experience love and compassion for other people that were not there before surrendering my heart to Him. Even though I still do not perfectly obey God in my efforts to love, I still experience the forgiveness, spiritual blessing, and love of God in my life.

If your heart is open to knowing the Truth; if your heart desires to know the truth and only the truth about you, others, God, and this life, God is more than willing and able to reveal the truth to you. God is good!

Every pearl of Truth that is revealed to us about the true nature of God will become precious when we seek to answer the questions, "Can I trust God?" and "What can we trust God for?" Our beliefs about God are foundational blocks of our spiritual life and faith.

To boil it all down, I believe God is good! (Psalm 100:5, 1 Timothy 4:). I believe God is Love! (1 John 4:16). Every desire and action of God in the past, in the present, and in the future is for our ultimate good (1 Timothy 4:4).

God's desire for us is a life of joy, a life of eternal hope and peace, a life without fear, a life filled with purpose and meaning, a life that is a constant blessing to everyone around us, a life that makes a positive difference in the lives of others, and a life that results in receiving temporal and eternal rewards!

Now I understand and have experienced myself that things happen in this world that can make us question if God is good and even question if He exists at all.

Millions of people are starving to death every day. People are living in extreme poverty, which can make their lives extremely difficult. People are being murdered all over the world by evil people. Injustices are being committed by the powerful over the weak.

Closer to home, sometimes our loved ones are taken from us with untimely deaths. People are born with birth defects. People suffer from lifelong diseases, pain, and handicaps that make life unfair. Sometimes in life, it seems as if everything that can go wrong does go wrong and for no clear reason. Sometimes we don't dare ask what else could go wrong because we fear we may shortly find out. Times like these tempt us to question the existence of a loving God who is good.

Those of you struggling right now with believing in a loving God, consider with me for a moment the alternative belief that those who question the goodness of God are right!

Consider that the bad things that happen to us in life are evidence that God is not good. Maybe God laughs at people in pain. Maybe the world is like some big dollhouse, and just for fun God zaps some people with diseases and causes others to get killed in accidents, floods, and earthquakes.

Can you believe this version of God? Can someone who believes this have any hope, any sense of peace, comfort, or security in life? Will they turn to this God for help?

Contrarily, I do not believe the terrible things we see and experience in life are evidence that God is not good, nor that God does not exist. Conversely, I believe God is good.

The reasons for suffering in this world are not God. I believe God mourns with those who weep and hates the pain and injustices that exist in this world. I believe all suffering is an accumulative effect of sin, a result of people living self-centered and selfish lives. They are a result of people making decisions that are not motivated by the Spirit of God's love.

One thing that makes sin so terrible is that the consequences of sin don't just affect the one who sins. Sin harms other people and causes them to suffer pain to various degrees physically, emotionally, psychologically, and even on a spiritual level.

In times of trouble, injustices, pain, and confusion, there are tremendous benefits to going back to focus on two foundational elements of Christian faith. I believe God the Creator exists and is good. I believe every desire and action of God for us is for our good. I stand on these two foundational elements of faith regardless of how the circumstances in my life may seem to say otherwise.

God is love, and everything God does is good. The reason for the pain and suffering experienced in this world does not lie at God's feet. Trusting in this truth gives me comfort and peace in times of confusion and suffering. We have a God who loves us unconditionally and cares about us. We have a God who understands and sympathizes with our pain.

I will say much more about the problem of the existence of evil in our world and the true nature of God as we continue. For now, I hope you can see that what we believe about God makes a huge difference in our views about what is happening in the world and what we can trust God to be and do! I believe God is good, and His love for us is unconditional. God is on our side.

Taking to heart and keeping in mind daily just these two beliefs—that God our Creator exists and that God loves us unconditionally—will unleash an unending stream of spiritual blessings into our lives.

We experience the presence of God and His love for us with each breath we take, in the light that surrounds us, in the warmth of the sun, and in the water we drink. We experience the unlimited knowledge and power of God in the details of everything God has created and maintains.

We can experience peace and comfort trusting that God is in control of all things and is demonstrating His love for us by daily meeting all our needs to live.

Our only comfort in life and death is that we are not our own but belong with body and soul, both in life and in death, to our faithful Savior Jesus Christ (Heidelberg Catechism Q&A #1).

Who do you believe God is? Why? Does what you believe enable you to trust Him in your life? Does what you believe enable you to be honest with God? What value would there be if God truly does love you personally and unconditionally? What can you trust God to be and do for you? Does your concept of God fill you with fear or peace?

THREE

Who Wants to Be a Spiritual Blessing?

———— FAITH KEY #3 ————

GOD DESIGNED US TO REPRODUCE HIMSELF
SPIRITUALLY, WHICH GLORIFIES HIM.

When God created mankind, he made them in the likeness of God. (Genesis 5:1)

And to put on the new self, created to be like God in true righteousness and holiness. (Ephesians 4:24)

For in him we live and move and have our being. As some of your poets have said, "We are his offspring." (Acts 17:58)

"Why do we exist?" This is a question everyone will ask themselves at some point in their lives. What is the purpose of our existence? Why are we here on this planet? Science has no answer for these questions.

If you don't know your purpose for doing something, how will you know if you are successful? When you don't have a purpose for doing something, you will not do it with any sense of passion, any sense of direction, or with any enthusiasm. If you don't know the purpose of your existence, how will you know if you are living a worthwhile and successful life?

If you believe there is a creator and believe our existence is more than some meaningless, random event, it naturally follows that our existence has meaning and purpose. It means that God had a reason for creating you and me and that we are valuable to Him!

If there was no purpose or reason for life, there also would not be any right or wrong in life; there would be no consequences to anything thought, said, or done. Nothing would matter if there is no God-given purpose and reason for living. Do what you will, for any reason you choose, and it just would not matter.

My own experiences in life, however, have made it clear to me that there are consequences to everything we think, say, and do. This is not just a belief; it is an experiential fact of life. We all learn about consequences in what we call the "school of hard knocks."

For example, on one occasion, I decided it would be a good idea to bring a small black squirt gun to school with me. While waiting for the bus at Sandy Hill school, I had it concealed in my coat pocket and would take it out from time to time to shoot someone.

Just as the bus was arriving, I pointed it at a big kid who was two years older than I was and a foot taller. Seeing the devious grin on my face, he said, "Shoot me with that, and I will kill you!"

At that point, seeing the bus arriving out of the corner of my eye, I sent two blasts of water flying into his face and dashed out the door toward the bus! When I got to the sidewalk curb, I turned around to see the enraged big kid charging me!

Suddenly, I felt something brush my jacket behind me, and a rush of unbelievable, depressing pain shot to my head! It was only later when I realized I had leaned a little too far back while avoiding my attacker. My left foot had stepped back down off the sidewalk curb unto the asphalt. The slight brush I felt on my jacket was the school bus, and a split-second later, the front tire of the bus had rolled up the back of my heel and stopped on my leg, just below my knee! That's when I learned the true meaning of the phrase "flatter than a pancake"!

Kids started yelling at the bus driver, "You are on Mark's leg!" Not believing what he was hearing, the bus driver, who happened to be my grandfather, got off the bus to look, and said, "Oh my!" and jumped back on the bus. He slowly backed down my leg, over my ankle and foot, and back onto the asphalt.

For the next month, I was lying on the couch with every pillow in our house under my leg, to keep my swollen ankle from throbbing when it was below the level of my heart. The only cool thing about it was the uniquely applied "tire tread tattoo" that was left pressed into the calf of my leg!

Life teaches us that there are good ideas and there are bad ideas. Shooting a big kid in the face with a squirt gun is a bad idea!

Some words and actions cause pain, and others produce pleasure. There are things we can say and do that hurt others, and there are other things that will benefit them.

When you realize there are consequences to each action in life, isn't it also logical that there are consequences to what we do with our lives as well? How we live our lives does matter!

The Christian faith teaches that we are all made in "the image of God" (Genesis 1:27, 5:1). We are made like God and made to be like God. We are created to act like God, talk like God, do the things God does, desire what God desires, and produce through our words and actions the same type of things God desires and produces. The desired result for each person created is to become a walking, talking spiritual blessing for other people.

Christian scripture tells us to "glorify God" in our lives (1 Corinthians 6:20, 1 Peter 4:16, Psalm 50:15). Through our words and actions, our purpose is to show the goodness of God and the greatness of His ways. We have each been uniquely made capable of sharing the blessings of God's spirit of love with others. This is doing the will of God. This is our purpose of existence.

We are also told that true worship is "doing the will of God in our lives" (John 4:23–24). Desires, motives, thoughts, words, and actions born of the Holy Spirit of God experientially show the greatness of God and His ways. Words and deeds rooted in God's love produce the fruits of the Holy Spirit. Experiencing these fruits is what makes life beautiful and good.

Consider an illustration of someone creating a game. The creator of the game defines the object of the game, how to play, and how to win. Playing a "good" game is determined by the creator of the game. The creator of the game likewise determines the goal and rules.

Similarly, what constitutes living a "good life" is determined by the Creator of life. Living a good life is living life via the ways and will of God. Experiencing the joy of life, experiencing life as God created it to be, living a successful life, and living a life in peace and harmony with others happens when a community of people lives according to the will and ways of the Creator.

The purpose of our existence is to reflect the goodness of the ways of God. We exist to glorify God. We exist to reproduce God's desires and ways in our lives. We are created to be "godly." We exist to duplicate God's attributes and reproduce His ways in and through our lives. We are created, likewise, with the need to be treated in godly ways.

Our created purpose is to reflect the spiritual nature of God in all we think, say, and do. This is living a "good life." This is becoming a spiritual child of God. This is fulfilling the purpose of our existence. This is what we will be rewarded for when we hear the words, "Well done, my good and faithful servant!"

This isn't an overly complicated concept. Reproducing God in our lives is done by desiring, thinking, speaking, and doing things motivated by God's Spirit to reproduce the effects of His Spirit of love in and through our lives. This is simple and straightforward. God made everyone with the ability to uniquely reproduce His nature in and through their lives. This is what makes us valuable to God and a potential blessing to others!

Everyone can speak the truth in love. Everyone can build others up. Everyone can be merciful, kind, and help others. Everyone can sympathize and show understanding with others. Everyone can listen to another. Everyone can "do unto others as you would have them do unto you." All these types of things are fulfilling our purpose for existing!

> Therefore, as God's chosen people, holy and dearly loved, clothe yourselves with compassion, kindness, humility, gentleness, and patience. Bear with each other

and forgive one another if any of you has a grievance against someone. Forgive as the Lord forgave you. And over all these virtues put on love, which binds them all together in perfect unity. (Colossians 3:12–14)

We should feel good about ourselves simply because we were created by God Almighty for this purpose. You should feel good about yourself because God has created you just the way you are with a unique ability to glorify Him. You should feel good about yourself because you can produce the blessings of God in a little different way than anyone else in the world can. God has created you to be a blessing to other people in ways that no one else can!

What does it all boil down to? When Jesus was asked, "When you look at the laws and commandments compiled by the scribes and Pharisees of the Jewish people, what does God expect from us?" Jesus's summary of all the law was:

> Love the Lord your God with all your heart, soul, and mind and love your neighbor as yourself! (Matthew 22:37–40)

That was it! That is what God expects from us. Loving God and your neighbor as yourself are what makes life enjoyable and what ultimately makes life worth living. Every person alive has a huge need to experience the fruits of the spirit of God's love.

This is the basis of what God will judge our lives on and reward us for. Our God-given ability to reproduce the desires and ways of God in our lives makes us a unique blessing created by God for others!

Think about this for a moment. What is it about your friends—the people you like—that makes you like and value them?

I like people who show in their words and actions that they like me! I am naturally drawn to people who make me feel good about me. I like people who say good things about me and to me. I like people who are honest with me, who help me, who are patient with me, who sympathize with me, who encourage me and build up my self-confidence! I like people who treat me kindly. Don't you?

That is the kind of person I want to be—a person who is re-creating the things of God through words and actions. That is the kind of person God has created me and you to be. This ability to uniquely reproduce the things of God in our lives makes us valuable to God and a potential blessing to everyone we meet!

What kind of person do you want to be? What do you think would make your life worth living? What things would you need to say and do to be that person who others will consider a real blessing?

We have all been created with the potential to be that person for others. Everything that we experience in this world God uses to equip and enable us to be that person spiritually!

What kind of person are you? What kind of person do you want to be? We were created to become the spiritual children of God!

FOUR

God Didn't Create Puppets!

> This day I call the heavens and the earth as witnesses
> against you that I have set before you, life and death,
> blessings, and curses. Now choose life, so that you and
> your children may live. (Deuteronomy 30:19)

In the previous chapter, I talked about how scripture teaches us that God created us in His image and how our purpose was to reproduce God spiritually in all the things we say and do. That is glorifying God.

Someone might ask, "If God wanted us to do His will and created us to do His will perfectly in our lives, why do we do so poorly at it? What went wrong? Did God do a bad job when He created us?"

Likewise, someone could argue that if God created us to do His will, to reproduce His desires and ways in our lives, why didn't He just create us so we could do nothing but His will perfectly?

Why didn't God just create the world and everyone in it, so they were already perfect? Why didn't God create us and the world so that this life would be paradise, right here, and right now, for everyone without any pain and suffering?

The issue I am addressing is the problem of evil in this world. It relates to the problems that develop from the existence of imperfections in this world that God created. If God created us, the world, and everything else, why does evil exist? Why do spiritual, physical, mental, and emotional imperfections exist? Why do we experience pain and suffering?

The answer lies in understanding all that is necessary when being created in God's image. To truly be created like God, it could not mean that we were created His puppets.

I believe being created in the image of God necessitates that He had to also create us spiritually free. To be like God, we had to be created with the ability to reason and make decisions on what we will desire, think, say, and do. Consequently, we likewise are also therefore responsible for each corresponding consequence of those decisions.

Let me explain. Nobody tells God what to do, and no one tells Him what He can and cannot do. God freely does what He does and desires what He does because that's what He wants to desire and wants to do. God's nature is to do good. God is a free spirit. God's ways are His ways because He wants them to be what they are. No one makes Him do anything.

Likewise, if we are created in God's image, if we are to be like God, we also had to be created with a free spirit that gives us the ability to decide what to do and what not to do. With this being true, we likewise are responsible for the decisions we make.

Let me illustrate it this way. If you discovered that your husband or wife only said that he or she loves you and only married you because he or she was forced to and had no other choice, would that be as valuable as if the person had done the same as a matter of free will? If you discovered your spouse was forced to love and marry you, I suspect that would take the joy right out of it! Love is not love unless we freely give it!

Another example is when someone is forced to say, "I am sorry." Does an apology have any value if someone is forced to give it? If he or she had no choice to do so? It would not be as significant as it would be if he or she was truly sorry for whatever was said or done.

To be truly made in the image of God we too must not be created without the ability of not being like God. God has not created us puppets that have no choice in what we desire, think, say, or do. God has created us spiritually free with the capability of doing whatever we want to do.

We can see this element of being created spiritually free in the Genesis story of the creation in the Christian Bible.

God told Adam and Eve not to eat of a tree called "the tree of the knowledge of good and evil" (Genesis 2:16–17). He even warned them that if they ate from this tree, they would die!

When Eve ate from this tree and likewise Adam ate of the tree, they both committed their first sin (Genesis 3). The Bible refers to this as the "original sin." They choose not to do the will of God and were responsible for the consequences of their sin.

Before eating from the tree of the knowledge of good and evil, all Adam and Eve's desires were generated from a spiritual union with the Spirit of God. Subsequently, all Adam and Eve's desires, thoughts, words, and deeds were rooted in the Spirit of God. They were spiritually one with God. Their minds were governed by the Holy Spirit. Their thoughts were continuedly rooted in the agape spirit of God's love, and so they desired to obey God's will, and thereby they did not sin.

It is significant that this tree was called "the tree of the knowledge of good and evil." Before eating from this tree, Adam and Eve did not decide for themselves what is good and evil. They mentally only knew what is good through their spiritual union with God. Likewise, their desires were in perfect harmony with God's desires.

When Adam and Eve ate from this tree, they broke the perfect harmony and communion of their spirits with God's Spirit. No longer did their spirit automatically flow with the desires and the ways of God. Up to this point the Holy Spirit decided for them what was right and what was wrong. After eating of this tree of the knowledge of good and evil, Adam's and Eve's spirits no longer were in perfect harmony with the spirit of God. Eating from this tree gave Adam and Eve "the knowledge of good and evil."

Adam and Eve could obey God or not obey God. They were spiritually free with the ability to choose whether they would eat of the tree of the knowledge of good and evil.

The consequences of disobeying God by eating of that tree were devastating. By this sin, they had broken their ongoing spiritual union with God. They were broken spiritually. They in effect unplugged themselves from the spirit of God. Suddenly they had to decide for themselves what was good and what was evil. God was no longer the sole conductor of the spiritual music of their hearts!

This Creation story in the book of Genesis tells us that after breaking God's commandment to not eat of this tree, Adam and Eve were suddenly afraid of God. Adam and Eve in fear subsequently tried to hide from God. They were ashamed of their nakedness and tried to cover themselves with fig leaves. They no longer were sure they could trust God. They now thought they should fear God.

As a part of the consequences for that sin, they could no longer live in the paradise of the garden of Eden. The ultimate consequence of that sin was death! They were no longer eternally connected to the life-giving Holy Spirit of God, so they, therefore, would die.

Taking responsibility for one's own choices and actions is almost a lost art today. We have become skilled at making excuses and blaming everything and everyone else for our poor choices. We like to justify the things we say and do by blaming others for the things they have said and done to us.

While these excuses may help others understand why we had the urge to say and do what we did, it does not negate the fact that we still had a choice. What others say and do does not make us do what we say and do. We are spiritually free, and we are also responsible for our choices.

Spiritual freedom and responsibility always walk hand in hand. When we make bad choices, we will reap the consequences of those choices. When we make good choices, we will enjoy the benefits of doing what is right.

God has created us spiritually free and responsible. He has not created us to be His puppets. God has created us with the ability to choose what we will think, say, and do. With this freedom of choice, we are also responsible for the choices we make.

The gravity of our decisions becomes even greater when we realize that the consequences of those decisions also affect the lives of others. The life we experience results from the collective decisions all people make.

Have you too learned that consequences exist to every choice you make? Are you mindful that when you make decisions, you are responsible for the consequences for each decision? How you and I affect the lives of people around us is directly related to what we decide to think, say, and do.

FIVE

It's Only Human Nature

FAITH KEY #5

HUMAN NATURE IS SPIRITUALLY BROKEN!

> Those who live according to the flesh have their minds set on what the flesh desires, but those who live in accordance with the Spirit have their minds set on what the Spirit desires. The mind governed by the flesh is death, but the mind governed by the Spirit is life and peace. (Romans 8:5–6)

Each of us needs to understand some things about human nature. How many times don't we hear someone say, "It's just human nature." Now when someone uses this phrase, it typically means that whatever was just said or done shouldn't be surprising. The idea is that it is natural for someone in that situation to say or do those types of things. Saying it is "just human nature" is saying it is a typical act of human nature.

A simple example of this might be when a person suddenly cuts you off with a car and forces you to veer off the road to prevent being hit by that car! The natural response would be fear and anger! It would be natural to want to cuss that person out. You might even want to send a message to that person with one of your fingers to let them know that you're not happy about what he or she just did. This is natural—typical of human nature. However, we must understand that just because something is typical of human nature doesn't mean it is the right thing to do.

The Bible teaches us some important things about human nature. I am hoping not to get too complicated here, but some terms that the Bible uses to describe our human nature we need to define to help us understand what the Bible teaches.

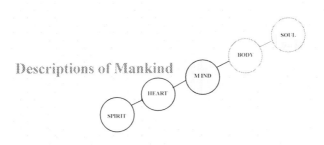

Descriptions of Mankind

SOUL
BODY
MIND
HEART
SPIRIT

» SPIRIT is the essence of God Given Life | HEART is the seat of our desires & will
» | MIND is the realm of thought | BODY is physical essence | SOUL is our total self

Terms about Human Nature

First, each of us has a spirit. It is that spark of life God gave us at conception that made us a living spiritual human being. We are spiritual beings. Our spirit is that part of us that can commune and communicate with God, who is the Holy Spirit. As I said earlier, our free spirit gives us the capacity to think, to have personal desires, to make decisions and choices as to what we will think, say, and do. We are self-determining, spiritual beings because we have a free spirit that enables us to reason, make decisions, and communicate those ideas.

The Bible also talks about our having a soul. We are living souls. It is commonly understood as that part of us that is unique to us even if we didn't have a body. At conception, when we are given the spirit or that spark of life from God, we become a unique living soul.

The Bible also talks a lot about each living soul having a heart. When the Bible talks about the heart, it is not referring to the physical organ of our body we know as the heart. Biblically, the heart is where our desires reside. It also talks about the heart as being the seat of the will. Our willingness to do something and our desires for something come from our hearts.

The Bible teaches us that we can choose the desires with which we fill our hearts. We can fill our hearts with the desires of God, or we can fill our hearts with the desires of the flesh. These desires will control or govern our whole thinking process. These desires determine the motives behind the act of thinking.

The condition of our heart determines whether we are willing to do something. It also teaches us that what we fill our hearts with has a significant impact on the way we think about things, and on what things we say and what things we do.

> Out of the abundance of the heart, the mouth speaks.
> (Matthew 15:18; Proverbs 4:23)

The Bible also talks about our having a mind. This is the same as we understand it today. The mind is our thinking world. The mind comprises everything that we think and remember.

And finally, it speaks of our having a physical body. The definition here is the same as we understand today. The Bible, however, also speaks of the influence of the body using the term *flesh*. When the Bible talks about people who are living according to the flesh, it means that they are allowing the desires of the body to be the primary influence on what they will desire and what they will think, say, and do. Living according to the flesh means we are allowing the physical wants and needs of our body to control or govern our thought processes.

It does not mean that physical wants and needs are evil in and of themselves, but God did not design us spiritually with our bodies in control of our decision-making process. We were designed to have our decision-making process under the control or governed by our spiritual desires. When we live seeking to satisfy the desires of the flesh, it will affect what we value, think, say, and do (Romans 8:5 NIV).

Now keeping these definitions in mind, let's talk about what the Bible says about human nature.

We need to look again at the Genesis story of Adam and Eve. Before Adam and Eve had sinned by eating from the tree called "the tree of the knowledge of good and evil," they were living in a spiritual union with God. The desires of their hearts were spiritually in harmony with the desires of God. Adam's spirit and God's spirit were one.

Through this spiritual communion with God, Adam's heart was thereby filled with the desires of God. When Adam's heart was filled with the desires of God, everything he thought, said, and did was in harmony with the desires and will of God. Adam's motives and desires were the same as God's motives and desires.

Also, because Adam's spirit was connected to the Holy Spirit of God, who is the source of life, there was no such thing as death. While he was connected spiritually with God Almighty, he would live forever. But like I spoke about earlier, to be truly made in the image of God, we could not be made simply puppets with no ability to make choices. We were created with a free spirit. In other words, we were created with the ability to decide for ourselves what to do and what not to do.

God had commanded Adam and Eve not to eat of the tree of the knowledge of good and evil. When they ate of the tree, they broke that spiritual union with God. A consequence of the sin of eating of this tree disconnected their spirit with the Holy Spirit of God; their spiritual union with God was broken. And because that sin broke their communion with God, who is the source of life, the penalty or consequence of that sin, just as God had warned, was death.

Everyone who sins is spiritually cutting themselves off from the eternal, life-giving Spirit of God. When we sin, we in effect unplug ourselves from the life-giving Spirit of God. Our spirit is no longer connected to the life-giving power of the Holy Spirit, and our hearts are no longer only filled with the will and desires of God. That sin broke our spiritual union with God and opened our hearts to the desires created through our physical bodies. The consequence of that sin was a spiritual disconnection with the life-giving Spirit of God, which inevitably results in death. A consequence of Adam's sin resulted in a spiritually broken human nature.

Adam's sin affected not only him but also his children and each descendant thereafter. Adam's "original sin" had a spiritual domino effect on everyone who came after him. Every person thereafter inherited that same spiritually broken human nature. Every single person therefore also is forced to deal with this inner conflict between the spiritual desires of God and the desires of the flesh (Genesis 8:21).

To better understand this, think of the typical laptop computer. If a laptop is plugged into an electric socket, which is the source of life for that computer, everything runs fine. Unplug that laptop from this source of energy that gives it life, and it is just a matter of time before the battery will go dead, and the computer will die. Comparably, by sinning, we spiritually unplug ourselves from our source of life and subsequently, being unplugged from the Holy Spirit, we will eventually die.

Another consequence of that first original sin was that Adam's heart was no longer automatically filled by the desires of God. With that spiritual union broken, Adam's heart was consequently now influenced by the desires of his body, or flesh, rather than just the desires of the Holy Spirit. After Adam's sin, the wants and needs of his physical body competed for control of his heart. To put it in biblical terms, Adam's heart was instead filled with the desires of the flesh that are at odds with the desires of the Holy Spirit (Romans 8:5 NIV).

In this way, down through every generation, our human nature remains spiritually broken. This spiritual brokenness results in the desires of our flesh warring against the spiritual desires of God to influence our hearts and minds.

In this state of spiritual brokenness, we must decide for ourselves which desires in our heart we will seek to satisfy. In this way, because of sin, our human nature remains spiritually broken. No longer is our heart only filled with the desires of God that produce thoughts, words, and deeds in harmony with the will of God and rooted in love.

> There is no one righteous, not even one; there is no one who understands; there is no one who seeks God. All have turned away, they have together become worthless; there is no one who does good, not even one. (Romans 3:10–12)

As we look at history through the biblical accounts of the Old Testament, we see that mankind became more and more self-centered and self-serving as they continued to live without this pure spiritual union with God. The more they satisfied the desires of the flesh rather than the desires of God, the more self-centered and self-seeking their hearts and minds became.

We see in the biblical account that it wasn't long before these self-centered desires of the heart led Cain to kill Able because of Cain's jealousy (Genesis 4, 1 John 3:12).

Living according to the desires of the flesh, people started to value experiencing physical pleasure more than doing what was righteous and good. As we read in the story about Sodom and Gomorrah, these two cities of people eventually totally ignored what was right and wrong in their pursuit of pleasure (Genesis 13:13, 18:20).

It is important to understand, living in this broken spiritual state, that we by nature are prone to be self-centered and selfish. Being influenced by the desires of the flesh, we discover we desire things that are contrary to the will of God. Left in this broken spiritual state, people are continually looking for ways to experience pleasure and avoid pain, often at the expense of doing what is right. Living in this broken spiritual state, our hearts desire to put our wants and needs ahead of others, and we are inclined to define "good" as simply whatever is best for us.

Now the reason I think it's important that you understand something about our inherited, spiritually broken human nature is not to give you another reason to feel bad about yourself but to give you a way to understand yourself and others better.

It is always important for us to understand and embrace the truth about ourselves if we want to understand others as well. The wise will always embrace the truth. The only way we can understand and sympathize with others is to realize and embrace the truth that we too struggle with the same things. The only way we can understand why we say and do things that hurt others is to understand our spiritual brokenness.

I have often said, half-jokingly, "Hey, give him a break. He doesn't mean to be irritating; he just doesn't know any better way." The joking aside, a profound Truth exists in that statement. Most people do not want to say and do things that are irritating and hurtful to other people. Additionally, most aren't even aware of what effect they are having on other people unless that person outwardly reacts to what is said or done.

When Jesus was dying on the cross, writhing in pain, He looked down upon those who were crucifying Him and said, "Forgive them, Father, for they know not what they do."

Jesus understood that the men who were killing Him didn't understand what they were doing. They didn't know that they were killing the only begotten son of God. Jesus understood that they were spiritually broken soldiers just doing their job and didn't understand the significance of what they were doing. Jesus, while hanging on the cross in pain, resisted satisfying the desire of His flesh for revenge and retribution and decided instead to satisfy the desire of the Holy Spirit to do the will of God and maintain His spirit of love. Jesus prayed, "Forgive them, for they know not what they are doing."

Have you ever noticed how much we change our thoughts and choice of words when we change the desires of our heart? Have you ever noticed the desires of your heart are often self-centered and selfish? It is only human nature. Our human nature is spiritually broken. Our hearts are spiritually disconnected with God, and, consequently, the desires of our physical bodies compete with the spiritual desires of God for control of our hearts.

Do you ever desire things that you should not desire? Are your thoughts ever self-centered? Do you say and do things you fully intended not to do? Do you also confess that you too, like others, appear to be spiritually broken?

SIX

A Light in the Darkness

FAITH KEY #6

THE LAWS OF GOD PROTECT US FROM OUR
SPIRITUALLY BROKEN HUMAN NATURE!

All who sin apart from the law will also perish apart
from the law, and all who sin under the law will be
judged by the law. (Romans 2:12)

If all people alive lived in a spiritual union with God and lived with
their hearts filled with the spiritual agape love of God, there would
be no need for laws. In this scenario, our hearts would be only filled
with the desires of God. Subsequently, every thought, every word, and
everything we did would be under the will of God and therefore rooted
in agape love.

Everyone across the world would continually generate peace, hope,
and love. All people would know and desire to do the will of God and
would likewise have the spiritual power to do the will of God. In such
a world, the Holy Spirit would orchestrate all creation in perfect living
harmony. Faith, hope, and love would be experienced within every
person's soul and would reign throughout the world! Every person
would live in the light of Truth, and there would be no need to teach
one's neighbor about God or about what he or she thought was right and

wrong. No one would have reason to hide their motives and thoughts about anyone or anything. What a wonderful world this would be!

This is a description of life in the spiritual kingdom of God. This is a description of what the experience of eternal life will be like when the spiritual kingdom of God rules in every heart.

This scenario, unfortunately, is not what we find in the world today. We are all spiritually broken. We do not live in a spiritual union with God Almighty. By nature, our hearts are not filled with the desires of God. The motives behind our thoughts, words, and deeds are often not rooted in God's unconditional love for other people. We say and do things that hurt other people and ourselves. In this spiritually broken state, we need the laws to protect us from ourselves.

Can you imagine what our lives would be like if there were no laws, and people would simply be left to say and do whatever they felt like saying and doing?

Without laws, do you think there would be more theft? More rape? More murder? Do you think powerful people would take advantage of the weaker? Do you think we would inflict more pain and suffering on each other because of our conflicting wants and needs?

Living with our spiritually broken nature in a lawless society would lead to all kinds of sin that would harm people beyond imagination. We see in the biblical account that it didn't take long for people living with a broken spiritual condition to sin more and more.

In the biblical narrative, we see that people living with this broken spiritual state became so evil that they didn't even remember God, let alone care about what His will was. In the story of Noah, we are told people had become so sinful and their hearts so self-centered and evil that God sent a flood to destroy them all (Genesis 6:5–9:25).

The Bible is filled with story after story about how our broken spiritual condition leads us into sinful ways and creates all kinds of painful consequences because of those sins. Even the Israelites, after witnessing their miraculous deliverance from slavery in Egypt by God, turned repeatedly to sinful ways because of their broken spiritual nature.

All history shows that mankind is quick to forget God, His will, and His ways. The natural consequence of our broken spiritual relationship with God results in self-centered acts of sin, the root cause of all pain and suffering in this world.

Knowing how self-destructive we could become because of our spiritually broken condition, God in His mercy did something to protect us. God revealed His will and ways to us by giving us His law. God graciously gave us His law, so we would not forget our Creator, so we would know what His will is, and so we would realize that His way to live is the only way to enjoy a blessed life in peace and harmony with one another.

Therefore, God gave us the ten commandments to help protect us from our sinful fallen nature. God spoke all these words to us through Moses on Mt. Sinai:

> I am the Lord your God, who brought you out of the land of Egypt, out of the house of slavery. You shall have no other gods before me.
>
> You shall not make for yourself an image, in form of anything in heaven above, or on the earth beneath, or in the waters below. You shall not bow down to them or worship them; for I, the Lord your God, am a jealous God, punishing the children for the sin of the parents to the third and fourth generation of those who hate me, but showing love to the thousand generations of those who love me and keep my commandments.
>
> You shall not misuse the name of the Lord your God, for the Lord will not hold anyone guiltless who misuses his name.
>
> Remember the Sabbath day by keeping it holy. Six days you shall labor and do all your work, but the seventh day is a sabbath to the Lord your God. On it, you shall not do any work, neither you, your son or daughter, nor your male or female servant, nor your animals, nor any foreigner residing in your towns. For in six days, the Lord made the heavens and earth, the sea, and all that is in them, but he rested on the seventh

day. Therefore, the Lord blessed the Sabbath day and made it holy.

Honor your father and your mother, so that you may live long in the land the Lord your God is giving you.

You shall not murder.

You shall not commit adultery.

You shall not steal.

You shall not bear false witness against your neighbor.

You shall not covet your neighbor's house. You shall not covet your neighbor's wife, or male or female servant, his ox or ass, or anything that belongs to your neighbor. (Exodus 20:1–17, Deuteronomy 5:6–21)

Now while hundreds of other laws can be found within the Bible, some of which are still relevant and others that are not, these ten commandments of God are important because they are the basis upon which most modern societies today base their laws.

I want you to understand that even man-made laws, backed up by threats of pain and punishment, are an effective means to control the desires of our fallen human nature. Our human bodies have an automatic defense system. When our hearts and minds are controlled by our body, we will naturally seek to enjoy pleasure and avoid pain. Laws are effective because even the most hard-hearted evil person will think twice about breaking the law if it means pain and some form of suffering will follow.

Giving us the law is not God's solution to our fallen, sinful nature, but it is a necessary means to manage and limit the amount of damage created by people living with a spiritually broken nature.

We need to understand that the laws of God are good because they are designed to reveal to us the will of God. They reveal to us what a person who lives in a spiritual union with God will and will not desire, say, and do.

Everyone needs a good sense of what is right and wrong according to God's will. This sense of right and wrong gives us a good healthy conscience in life. The laws of God are good because they serve us in a way very comparable to a light that is turned on in the darkness. They help us see what is and what is not the will of God. They reveal when our desires are not in harmony with the desires of God. The laws of God are good because they are designed to convict us of sin (Romans 3:20). The first step to solving any problem requires recognizing and accepting the fact that you have a problem.

Looking at the ten commandments from a spiritual point of view, we see they are a statement of truth about the true spiritual children of God. Those who are spiritually one with God—whose hearts are filled with the desires of God—"shall" or "will" not obey any other god before our Creator. They will not bow down to them or serve them.

Spiritual children of God will honor their father and mother; they will not murder, will not commit adultery, steal, bear false witness, or covet anything that is their neighbors'. This is important because anytime we know our desires are not in harmony with these commandments, we can also know we are not living in harmony with the Holy Spirit of God as a spiritual child of God would.

This is how we are "convicted" of sin; this is how we discover when we need to confess our sins to God and ask for God to forgive us and create within us a pure heart. A spiritual child of God who loves God with all his heart, soul, and mind and loves his neighbor as himself will already desire to fulfill these ten commandments. The motivation is not a law backed up with a threat of punishment but a spiritual desire of the heart.

The problem that remains, however, is that knowing the will of God doesn't give us the power to do the will of God in spirit and in truth. Knowing the will of God will only serve us as a light in the darkness revealing our need for further spiritual help from God.

SEVEN

Spirituality Is All About Heart

FAITH KEY #7

NO ONE CAN BE SAVED BY OBEYING THE LAW!

No one who relies on the law is justified before God, because the righteous will live by faith. (Romans 3:11)

It was not through the law that Abraham and his offspring received the promise that he would be the heir of the world, but through the righteousness that comes by faith. (Romans 4:13)

For it is with your heart that you believe and are justified, and it is with your mouth that you profess your faith and are saved. (Romans 10:10)

Laws help protect us from our selfish human nature, but they are far from the perfect solution to our spiritually broken condition. While shedding light on what the will of God is, the law does not give us the power, nor the desire, to do the will of God in spirit and in truth.

Just knowing what a spiritual child of God does and does not do, does not make us a spiritual child of God. Obeying the laws of God can also be used by "wolves in sheep's clothing" to fake being someone who is a child of God.

Remember my earlier example of someone being forced to say that they are sorry. Following some rule or law that says you need to say you're sorry is not the same as being sorry in spirit and in truth.

Truly obeying the will of God requires obeying from the heart, desiring what God desires, and loving as God loves—in spirit and in truth. Our spiritual condition is what is important. Having a heart filled with the spiritual desires of God is required!

Christ Jesus is the ultimate revelation of the will and ways of God. When Jesus was asked what the most important law of God is, or, in other words, what does God want from us, Jesus said:

> Love the Lord your God with all your heart and with all your soul and with all your mind. This is the first and greatest commandment. And the second is like it: Love your neighbor as yourself. All the law and the prophets hang on these two commandments. (Mark 12:28–34, Matthew 22:37–40)

Jesus taught that doing the will of God is a matter of the heart. Loving God, His will, and His ways, and loving our neighbor as ourselves is fulfilling all the laws of God. Loving in spirit and in truth is the fulfillment of all the laws of God (Galatians 5:14).

If you love your neighbor as yourself, you will not kill him, steal from him, or covet anything that is his. The whole point of the law was to give us an idea of what people would do and would not do when they love God and love their neighbor as themselves (Romans 13:8–10, Galatians 5:14).

We see in the teachings of Jesus that doing the will of God is a spiritual issue—a matter of the heart. In the Sermon on the Mount, Jesus said:

> You have heard that it was said to people long ago, you shall not murder, and anyone who murders will

be subject to judgment. But I tell you that anyone who is angry with a brother or sister will be subject to judgment. (Matthew 5:21–22)

We see here that Jesus understood that the commandment "You shall not murder" involves far more than simply the act of murdering someone physically. For Jesus, even being angry in your heart with a sister or a brother would make you guilty of breaking this commandment as well.

Jesus also said,

You have heard that it was said, you shall not commit adultery, but I tell you that anyone who looks at a woman lustfully has already committed adultery with her in his heart. (Matthew 5:27–28)

Jesus is teaching here that sin is more than simply the physical act of committing adultery. Jesus is teaching that sin is also a matter of the spiritual desires of the heart. Even looking at a woman lustfully is breaking this commandment and is a sin on the spiritual level.

When we let what Jesus is saying here sink in, we learn that sin is more than a physical act or deed. We see that sin includes more than simply something we say or do; it even includes more than something we might think. Sin includes all these things and the ungodly spiritual desires of our hearts.

When we consider these teachings of Jesus on the depth of sin, who could claim to be without sin? When we consider that sin includes the desires and intentions of our hearts, we are all sinners. (1 John 1:8–10) The root of sin is found on a spiritual level within our hearts.

The only way we can think, say, or do anything that is not sin is if we do so to satisfy a spiritual desire of God in our hearts. A pure heart, a holy heart, filled with the pure desires of God, can only be realized through an active spiritual union with God. This spiritual union, unfortunately, is the part that is broken in our human nature because of sin.

Understanding the depth of our sin and understanding that you and I are sinners is crucial for us to receive the salvation of God and live in an ongoing, eternal spiritual union with God. Embracing this Truth about our broken spiritual nature is one key to opening the door of our hearts to the salvation that God offers us through Christ Jesus.

One of the major spiritual problems among Christians today is a misunderstanding about the value and purpose of God's laws. We often misuse the laws of God to judge and condemn other people.

It is a misuse of the laws of God when used to justify and rationalize not loving someone because he or she has committed this sin or that sin. It is a misuse when used as a basis for sinful pride, where we use our carnal obedience to the law as a basis for believing and proclaiming that "we are better than you."

Now don't misunderstand me. Christians should desire to obey the laws of God. Every Christian should desire to do the will of God, for there are great rewards for doing the will of God, here in this world and in the world to come. It is a misuse, however, to use God's law as a tool to judge and condemn other people. It is a misuse of God's law to justify not loving another person because of his or her sin. Obeying the law of God is never a reason for boasting. Each of these misuses of God's law is sin and propagates the lie that obeying the laws of God is the way to salvation and the favor of God.

The apostle Paul in his letter to the Romans wrote:

> Therefore no one will be declared righteous in God's sight by the works of the law; rather, through the law, we become conscious of our sin. (Romans 3:20)

Jesus Christ Himself said to the Jews who were given the law of God by Moses:

> Not one of you keeps the law. (John 7:19)

It is important to understand the following point. Yes, if you obey all the laws of God perfectly, and do not sin, you will be righteous, and you will live eternally. However, no one obeys the laws of God perfectly. No one will earn salvation by trying to obey the laws of God. Knowing the laws of God will reveal to us something about the will of God, but through that same law, we will only become conscious of our sin and our need for God's mercy and forgiveness. Not one of us is good enough based on our obedience to the law to go to heaven.

Each one of us is a sinner. I am a sinner, and you are a sinner. We are broken spiritually, and we therefore sin. While the law of God will reveal to us the will of God and make us conscious of our sinfulness, we cannot earn our salvation by trying to obey the laws of God.

Each one of us needs a new heart that is spiritually reunited with God. Through this spiritual union with God, our hearts will be filled with the desires of God and spiritually empowered to overcome the impulses contrary to those of the Holy Spirit.

The good news: God has met this need for a new spiritual heart as well through Christ Jesus! Through faith, our hearts can desire what God desires! Read on. The good news about the blessings of God through Christ Jesus is just beginning! Even as God meets our physical needs in His creation, God desires to meet all our spiritual needs as well!

EIGHT

The Spiritual Path to Eternal Life!

FAITH KEY #8

JESUS IS GOD ALMIGHTY IN THE FLESH!

> What a wretched man I am! Who will save me from this
> body that is subject to death? (Romans 7:24)

These are the words of the apostle Paul after describing his struggle
with his spiritually broken nature. Who will save us from the spiritually
broken predicament in which we find ourselves?

> For God so loved the world that he gave his one and
> only Son, that whoever believes in him shall not perish
> but have eternal life. For God did not send his Son into
> the world to condemn the world, but to save the world
> through him. (John 3:16–17)

When I think of our spiritually broken predicament, it reminds me
of the old nursery rhyme about Humpty Dumpty. If you have ever read
the little story and have seen the pictures of Humpty, you will remember
that Humpty Dumpty was a little egg man whose body was an egg,
and he made the tragic mistake of sitting on a high wall. The nursery
rhyme goes like this:

> Humpty Dumpty sat on a wall,
> Humpty Dumpty had a great fall.
> All the king's horses, and all the king's men
> Could not put Humpty together again!

Poor Humpty! Once an egg is broken, who has the power and skill to put it back together again? Who can save him from his predicament?

The reason this little nursery rhyme reminds me of our spiritual predicament is that we too have a real problem fixing our spiritual brokenness. Because of our sin, we have broken our spiritual union with God and face the ultimate penalty of death. Who do we turn to, to fix our embedded spiritual brokenness? How can we be saved from eternal death?

Would you like to believe that our spiritual predicament is not hopeless? Would you like to believe a loving Creator out there is more than willing and able to put Humpty Dumpty back together again? The good news is God has created a way for us to be saved from our broken spiritual predicament and give us eternal life!

The heart of the Christian message is that God is loving and merciful. The ultimate demonstration of that love is that God himself came into this world as a man to give us a way for salvation! (Romans 5:8). God Almighty came into this world in the person of Jesus of Nazareth to establish a way for us to spiritually reunite with Him and thereby live eternally.

The Apostles Creed is a document put together to make a statement about what all Christians believe. This excerpt from that document talks about the Christian beliefs about Jesus of Nazareth:

> I believe in God, the Father almighty, maker of heaven and earth; And in Jesus Christ, his only Son, our Lord; who was conceived by the Holy Ghost, born of the Virgin Mary, suffered under Pontius Pilate, was crucified, dead, and buried.
>
> He descended into hell. The third day he rose again from the dead. He ascended into heaven and sits on the

right hand of God the Father almighty. From thence he
shall come to judge the quick and the dead." (excerpt
from the Apostles Creed)

That is a summary of what the Christian church believes about
Christ Jesus. A virgin, whose name was Mary, was impregnated not by
a man but by the Holy Spirit of God, and thereby, God Himself became
a human being (Luke 1:26–38, John 1:14).

The four Gospels of the New Testament and the early part of the
book of Acts tell us the story of the things Jesus (God) said and did
while walking among us on this earth.

Jesus was not born with the spiritually broken human nature that all
others inherit at birth from their fathers because He was not conceived
by the will of man. Jesus was conceived through the Holy Spirit, by the
will of God. Jesus became God in the flesh! (Colossians 2:9, John 1:14).

Jesus, however, was also fully human like any other person because
he was given birth by a woman, the Virgin Mary. He was a free spirit,
just like you and I, able to obey or disobey God (Hebrews 2:17).

Jesus was both God and a human man, at the same time. Jesus was
the incarnation of God as a man. Jesus was God in the flesh. Jesus was
God living beside us (John 12:45).

Throughout Jesus's life, He lived in a perfect spiritual union with
God. His spirit and God's spirit were one. The heart of Jesus, because
of this spiritual union, was filled with the love and the desires of God.
Therefore, Jesus could live a life without sin.

Because Jesus was God in the flesh, He revealed to us, through the
things He did and said, the true nature of God. He showed us what
God would say and do in all kinds of different situations. Through the
words and deeds of Jesus, God revealed to the world the Way, the Truth,
and the Life of God (John 14:6).

Living with this spiritual union with God the Father, Jesus also
showed the power of God. Just by speaking the words, Jesus healed the
sick, made blind men see, and miraculously called the crippled to stand
up and walk! (Matthew 11:4–5).

Jesus Himself said that if you don't believe me when I say that the heavenly Father and I are one, then believe me based on the miracles you have seen me do! (John 14:8–11). How could anyone do these things without possessing the power of God?

Living this perfect life in obedience to God, unlike everyone else, who had sinned, Jesus was not under the penalty of sin, which is death. Maintaining His perfect spiritual union with the life-giving Holy Spirit, there was no reason Jesus would ever die. The Holy Spirit is the source of life, and because Jesus maintained His spiritual union with the Holy Spirit, and thereby never sinned, there was no penalty of death before Him. The only way Jesus could die was if someone would kill Him!

Well, as we are told through the New Testament writers of the gospels, that is exactly what happened (Acts 2:22–24).

The religious leaders of Jesus's day, called the Sadducees and the Pharisees, absolutely hated what Jesus was saying and doing. The reason they were so upset was that if the people believed in Jesus and followed Him and His teachings, they would lose their religious power and influence over the Jewish people.

The Jewish leaders believed and taught that the only way to find favor with God was to know and obey the Jewish laws. They took great pride in their knowledge of the law and their efforts to obey them. They boasted about how often they went to the temple, how often they prayed, and how much money they gave to religious causes. They took great pride in knowing and obeying all the religious laws recorded in scripture.

They believed that because they knew and obeyed the laws of God more than other people did, they were holier than other people, and, subsequently, they believed God would bless them more because of it. The last thing they wanted to admit was that they too were sinners, broken spiritually.

They also believed it was their God-given duty to uncover and expose any sin that could be found in another person and then confront and punish the person for that sin. They believed and taught that if other people would become like them, become people who also knew and obeyed the law of God as they did, they too could receive the favor and blessings of God.

Jesus's teachings and ways, however, did not back up what the scribes and the Pharisees were teaching about God. He told the Jewish religious leaders that they were not holy. Jesus called them a "brood of vipers" (Matthew 12:34, 23:33).

Jesus said that the true child of God is not one that looks and acts like a child of God outwardly but is the one who obeys the will of God in spirit and in truth. The true child of God is the one who spiritually desires what God desires.

Remember the illustration I spoke of earlier, about someone who is commanded to say they are sorry. Obeying that commandment does not mean that a person is sorry in spirit and in truth. Likewise, living as a child of God requires a heart spiritually filled with the desires of God.

A good example of this spiritual conflict is found in a conversation between Jesus and the Pharisees about a woman that was caught in adultery who the Jewish leaders brought before Jesus (John 8:2–11). This woman was guilty, and both Jesus and the Jewish leaders knew that committing adultery was a sin and that the Old Testament scriptures taught that they should stone her to death. The Jewish leaders were there with other people ready to stone the woman when they asked Jesus what He thought should be done because of her sin.

Now, this was a trap, designed by these religious leaders to expose Jesus, who talked about the love and mercy of God, as a lawbreaker. Jesus continually emphasized the love and mercy of God toward sinners.

The scribes and the Pharisees conversely emphasized a vengeful God who will punish those who break His commandments. The scribes and the Pharisees hoped that this scenario would get Jesus to say something that would expose Him as someone who did not obey the laws of God, and someone, therefore, to whom the people should not listen.

After being asked what He thought they should do, Jesus paused for a moment, and His answer ended up exposing the scribes and Pharisees of being just as guilty before God as the woman they had brought before Him.

Jesus said, "Let any one of you who is without sin be the first to throw a stone at her." Slowly, as they thought about what Jesus said, every person there dropped their stone and walked away humbled. Jesus then turned to the woman and simply said, "Woman, where are they? Has no one condemned you?"

"No one, sir," she said.

"Then neither do I condemn you," Jesus declared. "Go now and leave your life of sin."

Jesus taught by His words and deeds that people could trust that God is a loving and merciful God. Jesus taught that each person needs to embrace the truth that he or she and everyone else is a sinner. He taught us that we should confess our sin before God and that God would faithfully forgive all those who will embrace the truth about themselves (1 John1:9).

Jesus taught that the entire human race was spiritually broken, and there was no hope for eternal life unless we could spiritually reunite with the source of life, which is God (John 2:2).

He taught that each of us needed to be spiritually reborn so that we could again live in spiritual union with God (John 3:3, 1 Peter 1:23).

This new spiritual union with God would enable us to fill our hearts anew with the desires of God and enable us to love God and others in spirit and in truth.

Jesus taught that one reason He came into this world was to create a way for us to be spiritually reunited with God. He came to establish a spiritual kingdom where God would reign over the desires of each person's heart (Matthew 4:17, Mark 1:15, Luke 4:43). He came to give us the ability to willingly fill our hearts with the desires of God and do His will in and through our lives.

The formal ministry of Jesus lasted for only three years. During these three years, Jesus continually talked about the love of God and the mercy He offers to all who look to Him. He healed the sick, made the lame walk, and made the blind see. Each miracle Jesus performed revealed the love and mercy of God toward sinners and the power of God within Him.

As time passed, and as Jesus's influence over the people increased, the religious leaders of the day grew increasingly angry with Jesus. They plotted and schemed repeatedly for ways to discredit Jesus and stop His message of a loving and merciful God. Each time they failed (Mark 14:55).

In the end, they decided the only way to silence Jesus was to kill him. So, they forcibly took Jesus to the Roman officials, alleging that He was a threat to the Roman Empire.

Pontius Pilate was the Roman governor in charge, and even though he could find no fault in Jesus, eventually succumbed to the demands of the angry crowds and commanded that Jesus would be crucified until dead upon a cross.

Jesus was crucified and painfully died on that cross. He died on a Friday, but on Sunday morning He rose from the dead! You can read the details of His trial, crucifixion, and resurrection in the New Testament from the accounts written by four of His disciples who were eyewitnesses (Matthew 27–28, Mark 15:16, Luke 23–24, John 18:28–20:31).

Jesus arose from the dead as a new creation. Jesus died a man who had never sinned and who had maintained a spiritual union with God throughout His life. He willingly paid the price of sin, with His death upon that cross, but because He was without sin, death could not hold Him, and He rose again to life from the spiritual place of the dead (Acts 2:24).

Through the life, death, and resurrection of Jesus Christ, God had paved a spiritual path through life and then through death as well that now leads to an eternally resurrected life. Through faith in and obedience to His heavenly Father, Jesus established the only spiritual path that leads through death to eternal life on the other side.

God sent Jesus to create this spiritual path through the place of the dead and back to life to show His unconditional love for us and His desire for everyone to be saved. God showed His unconditional love and mercy for all the spiritually broken by creating a way through Christ Jesus for us to be spiritually reborn with a heart that is spiritually in union with God's heart (John 3:16).

All those who desire to become the spiritual children of God, who desire to be and do all that God has created them to be and do, will receive this salvation and be empowered to live eternally as the spiritual children of God! (Galatians 4:7).

This story of God our Creator coming to earth, being born as a child named Jesus through the Virgin Mary, who then lived a sin-free life but then was killed unjustly by legalistic religious people, and then arose from the dead is an incredible story! God Himself coming to earth as a man to create a way to free us from the power of sin and the penalty of sin, which is death, and thereby provide us the gift of eternal spiritual life is a story that frankly is hard to believe, especially given the concept of the nature of God that many of us were taught!

People who simply live to satisfy their lust for pleasure, those who avoid pain at all costs, people who will hurt others to get what they want and need, those who didn't even try to know the will of God, let alone try to obey His will, are treated by God with love and mercy and offered forgiveness and salvation! This is an incredible story! How can we believe this is true? This sounds too good to be true. Do you believe it is true?

Ask yourself these questions: If this story of Jesus is true, would the Creator want you to know it is true? Do you believe God is willing and able to reveal the truth about Jesus to you?

Do you want to be a part of a community of people where your heart is filled with the loving desires and motives of God so that your every thought, word, and deed is within the will of God? Do you want the Holy Spirit to decide for you and everyone else what is good and what is evil so we can live in peace and harmony?

Jesus's message is that God is good, and that God is love. Jesus showed that our heavenly Father loves us and is willing and able to meet all our physical and spiritual needs to live. Jesus said, "I am God. I love you unconditionally, even though you sin. I willingly gave up my life so that you can be saved from death and be spiritually reunited with God. I love you and want to equip you to become the spiritual children of God. I want to empower you to become a walking, talking spiritual blessing of God for others to enjoy."

When you actively trust that the message of good news from Jesus is true, you will experience the blessings promised because the claims about Jesus and God are true.

For God so loved the world that he gave his one and only Son, that whoever believes in him shall not perish but have eternal life. (John 3:16)

And everyone who calls on the name of the Lord will be saved (Acts 2:21)

NINE

We Can Trust God with our Lives!

———— FAITH KEY #9 ————

FAITH UNLOCKS THE BLESSINGS OF GOD.

Without faith, it is impossible to please God because anyone who comes to him must believe he exists and that he rewards those who earnestly seek him. (Hebrews 11:6)

Years ago, a man traveled around the country putting on shows of death-defying events. On one occasion, he stretched a high wire across the river above the Niagara Falls. Thousands of people came out to see if he could walk across that wire above the waterfalls without falling to his death.

So, with thousands looking on, he slowly walked out onto the high wire and started carefully placing one foot in front of the other. Step by step he inched his way across the high wire. Especially when the wind blew, he would stop and waver, and the crowd would gasp, but he kept his balance and kept slowly moving forward.

When the man did finally step off the wire safely onto the shore of the other side of the river, the people began cheering him wildly for this great feat. The man yelled out to the people, "Did you like that?" And everyone shouted, "Yeah!" And the man yelled out again, "Now, who thinks I can walk back again to the other side?" And again, all the people excitedly yelled "Yeah, you can do it! Go for it!" With that, the man reached down and grabbed a huge wheelbarrow and rolled it out in front of him on the wire. The man turned and yelled out, "Great! Those who believe, I need a volunteer! Who will get into the wheelbarrow?" At that, the crowd fell deathly silent!

This little story does quite a lot to illustrate what the Bible means when it talks about Christian faith. Living with faith is more than just saying you believe something. It is not just a statement of belief. It is not magic. It is not some secret power or clever technique that makes God do what you want him to do.

Just saying you believe something is not what makes things happen. Faith is actively depending on a belief in spirit and in truth. Christian faith is actively trusting a Truth about God in the context of a real-life event. It is showing our beliefs by living our lives in that wheelbarrow!

The apostle Paul taught: "Christians are to live by faith, not by sight" (2 Corinthians 5:7). When instructing the Romans, Paul said, "Whatever is not of faith is sin" (Romans 14:23).

Scripture teaches us that "without faith, it is impossible to please God because anyone who comes to him must believe he exists and that he rewards those who earnestly seek him" (Hebrews 11:6).

We even see Jesus himself teach that the way things work in this world depends on your faith in God. While healing people, Jesus said to them, "according to your faith let it be done to you" (Matthew 9:29).

The bottom line is that God's desire has always been for us to believe and trust him in our lives for good things. Lies about the goodness and truthfulness of God become the basis for doubt.

Looking back again at the story of Adam and Eve in the garden of Eden, the devil attacked Adam and Eve's faith with lies about the goodness and truthfulness of God.

The devil was saying to Adam and Eve, "You cannot trust God; He's keeping something secret from you; the only reason He tells you not to eat of the tree of the knowledge of good and evil is that He doesn't want you to become as wise as He is." The devil was tempting them to believe that you cannot trust God to make all the rules and decide what you can and cannot do. By sowing these seeds of doubt about the goodness and truthfulness of God, the devil successfully tempted Adam and Eve to sin.

From day one, God has been looking for people who will willingly trust him to decide what is good and evil. God is looking for those who will put their faith in His power and love for them and let Him rule His creation (1 Corinthians 2:5).

Like a conductor of an orchestra, God is looking for people who will willingly trust him to guide them spiritually to play their part in bringing all God's creation into absolute peace and harmony. The only way we can all live in absolute peace and joy in life is for all of us to willingly allow God to spiritually fill our hearts with His desires. With our hearts filled by the Holy Spirit with the spiritual desires of God, our every thought, word, and deed will be within the will of the Conductor. We become the spiritual children of God. He is looking for people who will trust Him to make this come true for them and everyone else.

God is looking for people who will put their faith in Him to have the wisdom and power to meet all their physical and spiritual needs and thereby create absolute harmony throughout His entire creation.

The Bible, both the Old Testament and the New Testament, is a story about people being blessed by God through their faith in Him.

God blessed Abel, one of the sons of Adam, because he made an offering to God with faith that he would be blessed. Because of his faith in God's goodness, he was commended as righteous (Hebrews 11:14).

Most of you know the story of Noah. God told him it would rain for so long that the rainwater would rise so high that everyone would drown. Therefore, God told Noah to build an ark for himself, his family, and the animals to save them all from the coming flood. Noah believed God was telling the truth, and because of this act of faith, he and his family were saved from the flood (Hebrews 11:7).

The message of the stories of Abraham teach us that it was Abraham's faith that was accredited as righteousness by God, and therefore he became the father of all those who live by faith (Galatians 3:9, Romans 4:16).

Abraham's wife Sarah was also blessed by God because of her faith, "and by faith, even Sarah, who was past childbearing age, was enabled to bear children because she considered him faithful who made the promise" (Hebrews 11:11).

In the story of Moses leading the children of Israel out of slavery in Egypt, God blessed the people because of their faith in Him. "By faith, the people passed through the Red Sea on dry land; but when the Egyptians tried to do so, they were drowned" (Hebrews 11:29).

In the New Testament, we read story after story about how people were being healed by Jesus and His disciples because they had faith.

The message throughout the Bible is that being Christian depends on putting our faith in the loving goodness and truthfulness of God. Every blessing of God is received by grace through faith. Paul reminded the Ephesians, "For it is by grace you have been saved, through faith, and this is not from yourselves, it is the gift of God" (Ephesians 2:8).

The picture that Christ Jesus paints through His ministry is of a creator who loves His creation and desires to meet our every need physically and spiritually so that we might enjoy our life here together in peace and harmony to the fullest.

As Christians, living an abundant and victorious life filled with the blessings of God comes by daily living with faith in that God! (Galatians 3:9).

Jesus taught that the way things work in this world depends on trusting the truth of God's word (Matthew 9:29).

Understanding how Christian faith unlocks the blessings of God is important. I cannot overstate the importance of faith in God. Let me illustrate this by talking about how putting your faith in the Christian beliefs I've shared so far will result in blessings from God.

Now, remember my definition that Christian faith is actively depending upon a believed Truth. When that belief is objectively true, those that depend on that Truth will experience the blessing accordingly.

The first belief I stated was that God exists and that He is the one and only Creator of the heavens and the earth. When we put our faith in this Truth, actively depend on it being true, it will change how we think about this world, ourselves, and others.

Those who live with Christian faith and trust this Truth come to an experiential knowledge that they are not alone in this world. They know that the answer to the question "Is there anybody out there?" is yes! Those with faith in this Truth will experience the presence of God, see His glory in nature, and will know the comfort of not being alone. Why? It is because it is true; it is an objective Truth. God exists; He is spiritually here among us and will make himself known to you, and you will experience the blessings of this Truth as you put your faith in this Truth.

The second belief I stated was that God is good. Those who actively trust in their lives that this is true will receive blessings from doing so because it is true.

This belief likewise will change the way you think about things that happen in the world. For instance, when something happens in this life that causes people pain and suffering, some will ask why God did this. Those who trust in the belief that God is good will understand that God did not do this. God is good. No evil is in him. Every good and perfect gift is from God (James 1:17). The root of this pain and suffering is not God but human sin.

Everything God created is good because God is good (1 Timothy 4:4). He did not create evil, nor did He create the pain and suffering that always follows acts of evil. Sin, individually and collectively, is always the root cause of pain and suffering.

Add to these beliefs the foundational belief that we were created in the image of God, to glorify God, or to reproduce God in the things we think, say and do, and you will see the blessings of God continue to grow.

When you put your faith in this Truth, you will see the way you think about yourself and other people will change as well. You will find it a blessing to know that God Almighty, maker of heaven and earth, created you! Like everything else in God's creation, you are created with a purpose; you are valuable; you have an important part in making this life a blessing to others.

The same is true for everyone and everything else that God has created! God created the sun. The sun has purpose and value in this world giving us light and warmth. This part of God's creation is just one of the many necessary things we need to experience the abundant life God intended for us to experience. God created the bushes, plants, and trees with a purpose. They clean up carbon dioxide and produce oxygen, something again necessary for us to live. God created them with a purpose—they contribute a necessary part of what we need for us to live. God created us with needs, and He created the means to meet those needs as well.

Actively depend on the truth of these beliefs, and you will discover that this is true of everything that God has created.

Put your faith in the Truth that you are created in God's image to reproduce the good things of God in and through your life, and you will discover you have more than enough reason to feel good about yourself and more than enough reason to realize there is a significant meaning to your life. Trust this Truth, and you will discover that God will bless you with the ongoing hope that your life can make a positive difference in the lives of others.

Putting our faith in the belief that we are created in the image of God will also change our view of others. This means that every person who has received the spark of life from God has been created with a unique purpose and meaning as well. The old saying is true: "God doesn't make no junk!" If your name is Mark, Sue, Michelle, Bradley, Meagan, Kaleigh, Jaxon, Sherry, Riley, Rick, Kelly, Ryan, Stephanie, Lucas, Theodore, Oliver, Tiffany, Andrew, Jessica, Heidi, or Gary, whatever your name might be, you are created by God with a reason and an important purpose.

God has created you with a unique ability to be a blessing to others! Your life is important to God, and you will be a blessing to others if you trust God to help you become who He created you to be and do. Put your faith in this Truth, and you will discover more than enough reasons to feel good about you!

God wants you to experience and share these blessings with others. By putting your faith in this Truth, you will discover these blessings and become that blessing to others because you were created with the purpose and ability to be a blessing to others! You will experience the spiritual power of God flowing in and through you.

Are you beginning to see how actively putting your faith in these believed truths will compound the number of blessings you will receive and experience from God? Do you understand why, by putting your faith in God, you too will experience these blessings and more? That is because these Christian views are true!

We could go on all day rehearsing the many blessings of God that we will discover when we put our faith in him as our Creator—who is good and who created us to experience that goodness and share it with others. Remember also that we have been talking here about just three fundamental beliefs of Truth. The scriptures are full of truths about our loving Creator and the blessings He has in store for those who will actively put their faith in Him and earnestly seek Him (Hebrews 11:6).

Faith unlocks all the blessings of God. Get in the wheelbarrow of faith! God is pushing that wheelbarrow and will bless those who do! Actively putting your faith in these foundational beliefs of Christian faith and not just saying you believe them is crucial to building a successful and rewarding life!

TEN

Wisdom and Spiritual Power through the Gift of the Holy Spirit

---

FAITH KEY #10

WE ARE BEING EMPOWERED TO BECOME THE
SPIRITUAL CHILDREN OF GOD!

But the Advocate, the Holy Spirit, whom the Father
will send in my name, will teach you all things and will
remind you of everything I have said to you. (John 14:26)

For those who are led by the Spirit of God are the
children of God. (Romans 8:14)

Our gift of salvation through Jesus Christ involves much more than just
the promise of eternal life! The gift of the Holy Spirit is also given to
us by our Creator as part of that salvation through the life, death, and
resurrection of Jesus Christ (John 14:26, Galatians 3:14).

The gift of the Holy Spirit is the power of God that gives us the
ability to willingly become the new creation He desires, the spiritual
children of God (Galatians 3:26, 4:6; Romans 8:14, 16, 23).

We need to remember here that our spirit is that piece of the Holy
Spirit that gives our bodies the spark of life. Our spirit is our life-giving

power source (Job 33:4). Our spirit makes us uniquely who we are; it gives us the ability to reason, and it is that which makes us a unique living soul (1 Corinthians 2:11).

However, as we discussed earlier, our spirit became disconnected from God spiritually because of sin. Sin disconnects us from our intended spiritual oneness with God—that ongoing spiritual union with God that purifies the desires of our hearts.

The good news of Jesus Christ includes this empowering gift of the Holy Spirit. It means that through Jesus Christ we have been spiritually reconnected with God—the source of life. It means with this gift of the Holy Spirit we can experience an ongoing spiritual communion with God Almighty. It means we can walk and speak with him continually throughout our lives. Through this gift of the Holy Spirit, we can now authentically fill our hearts with the desires of God and thereby think the kind of thoughts that are characteristic of God's unconditional agape love (Acts 15:8).

Through the Holy Spirit, we have been given the spiritual power needed to love God and our neighbor as ourselves in spirit and in truth. The true Christian does not obey God because he must or because he fears punishment; he obeys because the Holy Spirit has enabled him to love in spirit and in truth (Romans 8:15).

Through the Holy Spirit, God writes His law within our hearts. Everything we need to know about God, about ourselves, and about the life that He has called us to live comes through the revealing power of the Holy Spirit (Ephesians 1:17, 1 Corinthians 2:10–13).

Jesus lived His life with incredible wisdom and power! Jesus showed the spiritual power to overcome all temptations and live a sinless life. He spoke words of truth that healed the hearts of others, that filled them with hope, and that renewed their faith in God. He showed the power to cure those who were sick and heal the lame. He showed a love for others that even enabled him to forgive those who were killing Him while dying on the cross. The power that enabled Jesus to do all these things was the Holy Spirit.

The same spiritual power that equipped Jesus to be and do all that He did is given to us through His gift of the Holy Spirit. We receive this gift not because we deserve it based on our righteous works, but because of the love and mercy of God toward us (2 Timothy 1:9, Titus 3:5).

The life-changing implications of this gift of the Holy Spirit cannot be overemphasized. With this new spiritual communion with God, that spiritual oneness with God that Jesus gives us, we can now change the desires of our hearts. We can now love God and others in spirit and in truth!

We see part of the importance of this gift when we think about the teaching of scripture that says, "It is out of the desires of the heart that the mouth speaks" (Luke 6:45).

When we think about other people and then mentally decide to say something to them, what we think about them and what words we speak to them are influenced by the desires of our hearts. The desires of your heart determine what we say to others and how we speak to them. The motives behind all human thoughts are determined by the desires of our hearts.

The intentions, the motives, and the purpose of the whole thinking process that formulates ideas, words, and actions are determined by the desires of our hearts. The ability to say something loving, uplifting, and that will bless other people depends on the desires of our hearts. Conversely, if our hearts desire to glorify ourselves, the words we choose and how we say those words are also determined by that desire within our hearts.

Let me illustrate the influence of the desires of the heart with a few examples. Have you ever noticed that when people are in a group, two people can listen to the same thing that another person says, and they respond in different ways?

One person might criticize the things he just said, while another person may compliment him for what he just said. One response might embarrass him and make him wish he had never said a word; while another response might make him feel appreciated for sharing that statement honestly.

What causes these entirely different responses to come out of two people when they both heard the same thing being said? The desires of the heart cause two people to think in different ways about what the person has to say.

The desires of the heart change the motive behind the words in response to what another person said. If your heart desires to hurt that person, you will develop ideas and select words that will do so.

If your heart desires to make that person feel appreciated and loved, you develop ideas and words to do so. So, when you understand this, how fantastic it is to receive the gift of the Holy Spirit—to be given the ability to fill your heart the desires of God!

With this gift of the Holy Spirit, we have been equipped to become the spiritual children of God (Romans 8:14). We are enabled to share God's motives and thereby think like and speak like God to others. It quickens our minds with ideas that are loving, merciful, compassionate, understanding, and uplifting, just like God! With the Holy Spirit, He enables us to speak the truth in love. The ability to treat others in a godly way requires having the same desires of God toward that person and for that person. The gift of the Holy Spirit gives us the ability to possess the same desires of God.

Have you ever had a desire that you know you should not desire? What I am asking is how do you stop desiring something that you do desire? How do you desire something that you should desire but you do not desire? The power to change the desires of our hearts comes through the gift of the Holy Spirit. Trust God to fill your heart with His desires and His will!

I am not talking here about becoming a religious person, as helpful as that may or may not be. I am talking about a living relationship with God, where He enables and equips us to willingly be, say, and do everything He wants us to be, say, and do.

Christians do not obey God because they must or because they fear getting punished if they do not. Christians obey God because through the gift of the Holy Spirit they now want to obey Him in spirit and in truth. We can and want to love God and love our neighbor as ourselves in spirit and in truth.

Everything our Creator wants us to become and do as a person, He also equips and empowers us to be and do through the gift of the Holy

Spirit. This gift of spiritual power is available to every single person God has created through the salvation Jesus offers by grace through faith.

So much more needs to be said about this supernatural power that comes through the gift of the Holy Spirit, but it would be better said in a separate book on this topic. For more good news about Christian spirituality, go to my website for more information about my book entitled *Let's Get Spiritual.*

ELEVEN

Ushering in the Kingdom of God!

FAITH KEY #11

EMPOWERED TO REVEAL THE NEW SPIRITUAL
REALITY OF THE KINGDOM OF GOD!

> For we are God's handiwork, created in Christ Jesus to
> do good works, which God prepared in advance for us
> to do. (Ephesians 2:10)

One thing I think about from time to time is, "How will I feel about my life when I am lying on my death bed?" I mean, when I am about to die, will I look back at my life and be at peace with the things that I have said and done? Will I be at peace with the spiritual fruits that have been produced through my life? Will I be confident that when I come face to face with God, I will hear him say, "Well done, my good and faithful servant!" (Luke 19:17).

Quite early in my life, I embraced the weight of the reality that each one of us has only one life to live. Given that fact, it became clear to me that it is important to do it right.

Likewise, it became extremely important to me to know and focus on what we are here on earth for. I concluded we must be here for a reason. I believed there are a right way and a wrong way to live one's life, the evidence being the consequences that always result from the decisions we make. I concluded it was important to be and do what God created me to be and do in my life because consequences exist to each decision we make.

I concluded that the only way you can feel satisfied and confident that you are living a meaningful and successful life is if you know what you are created to be and do here. The only way you can be confident that God will say, "Well done, my good and faithful servant," is if you have a good idea of what God wants you to be and do in this life.

This is especially true for knowing what a Christian is, and what a Christian is created to be and do in his or her life. When a person is spiritually born again through Jesus Christ, it does not just mean that his or her sins are forgiven, and that person will receive eternal life. If that were the case, if eternal life were the only end goal of our existence, why wouldn't God just rapture us into paradise right then and there as we surrender our hearts to Him? The fact that born-again Christians remain here clearly demonstrates there is more to God's plan than just receiving eternal life.

When a person becomes a Christian, God fills him or her with the power of the Holy Spirit for a specific reason and goal in mind. The gift of the Holy Spirit enables us to increasingly live as spiritual sons and daughters of God in this world—members of the kingdom of God. The Holy Spirit then begins to enable us to experience our new spiritual reality in Christ Jesus.

When spiritually born again, the Holy Spirit equips us to help Him accomplish His plan and His goal for this creation. As such, we are learning to know and do the will of God as members of His spiritual kingdom in this world.

When the disciples of Jesus asked Him to teach them how to pray, Jesus said, "Our Father, who art in heaven, hallowed be thy name. Thy kingdom come, thy will be done, on earth as it is in heaven" (Matthew 6:10, Luke 11:1–2).

When we read the Gospel accounts of the life and ministry of Jesus, we find Jesus talking often about the "kingdom of God" and the "kingdom of heaven."

When Jesus's disciples heard Jesus talking about establishing the kingdom of God, they mistakenly thought Jesus was talking about making the children of Israel the supreme rulers of this world. The disciples thought that Jesus was talking about an earthly kingdom where Jesus would be king and where they, as the disciples of Jesus, would also become rulers with various levels of power over the whole world.

They were looking for and hoping for a Messiah that would overthrow the reign of the Romans over them. They were looking for a Messiah that would rule over all nations of the world as an earthly king.

Jesus had to constantly remind them that the kingdom He was establishing was not earthly but a spiritual kingdom. The kind of kingdom that Jesus was establishing was a spiritual kingdom where the rule of God would reign spiritually in the hearts of His people. The power of salvation and this spiritual kingdom is not the threat of eternal damnation of death based on obedience to the laws of God. The power of salvation and the kingdom of God is the unconditional love of God for us revealed through Christ Jesus!

It is a kingdom where people are not be controlled by laws or threats of punishment or by human might. In this new spiritual kingdom, people will willingly do what is right and what is loving because that is what they now spiritually desire to be and do.

People who enter the kingdom of God willingly desire the spiritual love of God to influence their thoughts, words, and deeds. After experiencing the unconditional love of God through Christ Jesus, they no longer will see obeying the will of God as a burden but as a privilege and joy of their new spiritual relationship with God.

In this spiritual kingdom, people look to God in faith to enable them to live Christ-like lives that powerfully create spiritual blessings in the lives of others. It is a spiritual kingdom where people speak the truth in love and thereby enable the Holy Spirit to use those words to heal the hearts and minds of other people.

As Christians, we are called to usher in this kingdom of God! It is a spiritual kingdom that is already established by Christ Jesus. It is a powerful spiritual kingdom that already exists here and now. It is a kingdom that has dominating power over principalities and powers of darkness here and now! It is a spiritual kingdom that has the power to change people's hearts and minds and enable them to live in peace and harmony with God and with one another!

Let there be no doubt about it, the spiritual kingdom of God is more powerful than any other power within this world. This spiritual kingdom of God is the same kingdom that we will experience eternally in heaven. The reason that heaven is referred to as paradise is that the spiritual reign of God will exist within the hearts of every person in heaven. The reason our experiences there will be paradise is that the hearts of every person there will be filled with the unconditional agape love of God. It is this agape love that will cause us to desire the things of God, that will cause us to think the thoughts of God, and that prompts us to do the things of God. Everyone will be living in spiritual harmony with God Almighty and with one another.

What Jesus is calling us to be and to do as Christians is to help him reveal the reality of the power of this spiritual kingdom of God that He lived, suffered, and died to establish. We are spiritually empowered to demonstrate within our lives—within the things that we say and do—how much better His way of life is than anything else that one can experience in this world.

God's plan to change this world is not through worldly power or through laws that compel people to do what He wants. God's plan to change the world is through the hearts and minds of people who offer themselves up willingly to the influences of the Holy Spirit.

God plans to heal and change each person from within his or her heart. God will change each person in this world by allowing him or her to experience the benefit of His unconditional love for them. The power to change people's lives for the good is found in every word and deed that is spoken and done in the spirit of agape love.

Christians usher in the kingdom of God by allowing the spiritual reign of God to influence their hearts and minds while living in this world. The spiritual reign of God is being revealed each time the unconditional love of God is being shared with another.

This is what it means to live *in* the world while not being *of* the world.

You do not separate yourself from people of the world geographically or physically; you live where they live and interact with everyone. The difference is that while you are with others; you do not think as the world thinks; your thoughts and words are born and influenced by the spiritual desires of the Holy Spirit! The spiritual kingdom of God is active where truth is embraced and where words and deeds are being shared with agape love.

As Christians, with the power of agape love ruling our hearts, we are called to show the power of this unconditional love to each person we meet. Like Jesus, we too are called to give people hope, to assure people of God's love, to convince people that God can be trusted to control their lives.

God calls us to let people experience the unconditional love of God through how we treat them. We are to show people this spiritual way of living, even as Jesus showed us that way. We too are to share the healing power of God's agape love by becoming vessels of God's blessings to everyone we meet.

The only thing that will heal hardened, broken hearts is the unconditional agape love of God. The best way to experience the healing power of God's love is for someone to love us unconditionally. The best way to know the value of forgiveness is to experience being forgiven.

Our lives will be meaningful and satisfying if we live our lives in a Christ-like way. As Christians, we have been given a new spiritual life to share the same unconditional love that God has shown us in Christ Jesus with every person we meet. In doing so, we will reproduce the fruits of the Holy Spirit through our lives. By treating people in a Christ-like way we will be giving them peace, we will be giving them hope, we will be building them up to feel good about themselves and likewise desire to be a spiritual child of God.

Sharing this love with others has the power to heal their hearts so that they too can dare believe in a God who loves them and will save them. Nothing is more meaningful and satisfying than to live a life for God that is a blessing to other people.

When we are lying on our deathbeds, the only way that we will have that true sense of satisfaction and accomplishment is if we have fulfilled our call to usher in the spiritual kingdom of God within our lives. The way to ensure that we will hear the words "Well done, my good and faithful servant!" is by surrendering our every thought, word, and deed to the spiritual reign of God and His unconditional love.

TWELVE

Arm Yourself for Spiritual War!

FAITH KEY #12

YOUR FAITH WILL BE TESTED.

> For our struggle is not against flesh and blood, but against the rulers, against the authorities, against the powers of this dark world and the spiritual forces of evil in the heavenly realms. (Ephesians 6:12)

I have previously stressed that every blessing of God revealed to us through Christ Jesus is received by grace, through faith. This good news of Jesus Christ is incredible! Our salvation, the forgiveness of sins, the promise of eternal life, the gift of the Holy Spirit, which empowers us to become the spiritual children of God and equip us to usher in the kingdom of God, are all received by grace, through faith.

It all seems so simple! "You mean to tell me that I don't have to do anything to get God to love me? God already loves me unconditionally, promises me salvation, and offers me these spiritual gifts?" The answer is a resounding yes! Trust in the truth of these promises, and you will receive and experience it all!

However, I do not want to leave you unaware. Do not be surprised. As soon as you jump into that wheelbarrow of Christian faith, powers of darkness will seek to stop you from living with an active Christian faith. Your Christian faith will be tested and purified!

You will discover as you roll out on that high wire of faith, you have entered a spiritual battle that seeks to control your heart and mind. You will discover principalities and powers of darkness; evil spirits and demons will come out of nowhere to stop you from living with Christian faith (Ephesians 6:10–12). Their goal will be to use everything possible to get you to doubt the saving power of the unconditional love of God shown us in Jesus. They will try to get you to believe you are a naïve fool to leap into that wheelbarrow of Christian faith.

I will not enter a debate here about the existence of evil spirits and demons except to say that we see in the gospel accounts of Jesus's life and ministry that He believed in the existence of Satan, evil spirits, and demons. We are told that Jesus confronted evil spirits and demons and cast them out of people as He sought to bring them healing (Luke 7:21, 11:14; Mark 1:32–39; Matthew 8:31, 17:18).

These principalities and powers of darkness use their power to get us to doubt the new spiritual reality that we have received by grace through faith in Christ Jesus. Satan will try to keep you from trusting and loving God with all your heart, soul, and mind and keep you from loving your neighbor as yourself. His goal is to destroy your Christian faith and prevent you from experiencing the blessing of God's spiritual rule in your heart.

Satan's favorite weapon is to use lies about God and about you and others to convince you that God cannot be trusted and that the good news of Jesus Christ is not true.

Satan will point to bad things that happen in your life and suggest in your mind that this is proof that God does not love you unconditionally, that you are not saved, and that God won't do anything for you. If possible, he will use disappointing events of your life to convince you that God does not even exist at all!

Another popular tactic of Satan is to use your sins as the basis to get you to doubt God's love for you. He wants you to believe that because of your sin, you will not receive the spiritual blessings that come through

Christ Jesus. He especially loves using others to judge and condemn you for your sin.

These beliefs are lies! The truth is that God loves us unconditionally while we are yet sinners. Jesus showed this unconditional love when He was being unjustly and painfully killed on the cross, and He said, "Father, forgive them, for they do not know what they are doing" (Luke 23:34). He likewise showed that same love when He said to the thief being crucified on a cross with Him, "Today, you will be with me in Paradise!" (Luke 23:34, 43).

Another favorite tactic of the devil is to use the things other people say and do to convince us that we are unlovable and of little or no value to God or others.

Look at the number of young people today who come to believe, because of the things that others have said to them, that they are unlovable, have no value, and have little or no hope for a future. They become victims of the lies of other people. They have either not heard, or they have not believed the Truth that they are created by God, loved by God, and have been given a life that has meaning and great value. They have not lived with the peace and hope that comes from knowing they can become a walking, talking blessing to other people and that they are uniquely created to bless others.

Likewise, be especially aware of legalistic, carnal minded religious people. They are the modern Pharisees of Christian churches today. Their carnal minds are still controlled by the same evil spirits that motivated the Pharisees of Jesus's day to get Jesus crucified on a cross. These legalistic religious people are still the favorite tool of the devil today!

Carnally minded people are opposed to the things of the spirit. They do not understand the things of the spirit, nor can they. Their minds are controlled by the flesh and not by the Holy Spirit (Galatians 5:17). Satan uses them to sow seeds of doubt, strife, and division. The bottom line is that they do not believe in the power of the unconditional love of God to change or save them and other people.

Carnal-minded people believe that they earn the favor of God by their religious works and by their efforts to know and obey the laws of

God. They believe the number of times they attend religious activities, the way they pray in public, and the amount they give to the poor is being a witness for God. The reality, however, is that the only thing they are being a witness of is their religious pride and self-righteousness (Luke 20:46).

These legalists believe they are being good servants of God by pointing out the sins of others and by condemning and punishing them for those sins. They believe that by heaping shame upon others they will lead others to repent and try to obey God as they do. Their carnal minds will not allow them to see or understand that it is only the unconditional love of God shown us in Christ Jesus that has the power to change the hearts and minds of people.

The point I am making here is that the battle for the hearts and minds of people is spiritual. The battlefield for this war is in your heart and mind. We fight not against flesh and blood, but against principalities and powers of darkness (Ephesians 6:12). Other people are not our enemy but the spiritual powers that use and seek to control them.

To win these spiritual battles, we need to work with the Holy Spirit to renew our minds, so that all our thoughts are in harmony with our new spiritual reality in Christ Jesus (2 Corinthians 10:5). Every thought we have that contradicts the good news of Jesus Christ will be used by Satan to destroy our Christian faith and prevent us and others from experiencing the spiritual blessings promised.

This is one reason building our lives on the solid foundations of the spiritual beliefs of the Bible is so important! Jesus said it will be done to you according to your faith. Knowing what we believe and why is a crucial part of the process of spiritually renewing our minds to conform to our new reality in Christ Jesus (Romans 12:2). We need to know and teach our children what our new spiritual reality in Christ Jesus is.

Look at the foundational belief that God exists, that He is our heavenly father, and that He is the Creator of all things. This belief is crucial to all other Christian beliefs. If Satan knocks this belief out, everything else contained in the Christian worldview falls with it.

If God is not good, filled with love and mercy toward us, we live with no hope. We live with no assurance of salvation.

It is important to understand that we have been made in God's image. We have therefore been created with a purpose, given a life that is valuable to God and others. The fact that we have been made in the image of God means we can reproduce in our lives the things of God. Our thoughts about ourselves and others need to reflect this reality.

No, we have not been created puppets but are created by God as free spirits with the ability to reason and make our own choices. This means we should always be mindful that we will be held responsible for the decisions we make and must willingly seek to become godly in spirit and in truth.

We must realize that sin is the problem, that we all are spiritually broken because of sin, and that the penalty of that sin will be death.

Yes, the laws of God are a blessing in that they protect us from the depth of the pain and suffering our spiritual brokenness can cause, and they will convict us of our sin and reveal our need for spiritual help. We need to remain mindful that trying to obey the laws will not save us or win the favor of God. Jesus provides the only solution for that spiritual brokenness: a spiritual rebirth through faith.

Jesus was God in the flesh, and He alone revealed to us the true and full nature of God—that "God is love" (1 John 4:8). He alone has paved a spiritual path to eternal life. We must renew our minds to reflect the loving nature of God that Jesus revealed in His life.

We need to know what we believe and why so that the Holy Spirit can empower us to bring our every thought into conformity with our new reality in Christ Jesus (Romans 12:2).

Now when I raise the point here that when we seek to live with an active Christian faith, powers of darkness will break loose to stop us, I am not saying we, therefore, need to be afraid. On the contrary, the spiritual war is already over, and the unconditional love of Christ Jesus has already brought the victory when Jesus arose from the dead (1 Corinthians 15:57).

Agape love has already won! No principality or power of darkness, no evil spirit or demon has any spiritual power or authority over the power of the gift of the Holy Spirit that we receive through faith! (Philippians 2:9,10).

The apostle James said, "Resist the devil and he will flee from you!" (James 4:7). He will flee not because we have established some power or authority in the spiritual realm ourselves, but because we have been given the ability to wield the power and authority of the Holy Spirit in Christ's name. We are victorious over all the schemes of the devil when we by faith trust the truth of God's word to win our spiritual battles (Ephesians 6:11, 1 John 5:4).

Every person who lives with Christian faith will have his or her faith tested. Events you experience in life will be used by Satan to try to destroy your faith and take away your experience of the promised blessings of faith, but God will use those same events to strengthen and purify your faith in Him.

Throughout the New Testament, Christians are encouraged to "stand firm in the faith"! (1 Corinthians 16:13, Luke 21:19, 1 Peter 5:12). The truth is that God is almighty; His wisdom and power are limitless. His love for us is limitless. Stand firm in your faith in the power and love of God because all the blessings of God are received and experienced by grace through faith!

THIRTEEN

Focus on Heavenly Treasures!

WE ARE REWARDED FOR OUR SHARING AGAPE LOVE!

> Do not store up for yourselves treasures on earth, where
> moths and vermin destroy, and where thieves break
> in and steal. But store up for yourselves treasures in
> heaven, where moths and vermin do not destroy, and
> where thieves do not break in and steal. For where your
> treasure is, there your heart will be also. (Matthew
> 6:19–21)

It is not always easy to usher in the kingdom of God. It is not always easy to do the will of God in this world. It can be difficult to love others as ourselves.

We begin to realize how difficult when Jesus says it includes "blessing those who curse you" and "forgiving those who sin against you." But again, we need to hear the good news of Jesus Christ! There will be great rewards for those who do the will of God in this world here and now (Ephesians 6:8, Colossians 3:24, Hebrews 11:26, Revelation 22:12).

Loving people with the unconditional love of God can be made exceedingly difficult by other people in this world. People who curse us and who do all manner of evil against us are difficult to love. The impulse of our old fallen nature was to do unto others as they have done unto us. It is a natural reaction in our old human nature to curse those who curse us. Blessing those who curse us just does not seem to make sense.

It was quite a different spirit that prompted Jesus to say while hanging on the cross, "Father, forgive them, for they do not know what they are doing" (Luke 23:34). Jesus assured us that this spiritual struggle against the flesh to do the will of God in spirit and in truth will be greatly rewarded in heaven.

What is important to remember is that each spiritually motivated act and word of love to another person brings with it an eternal reward. These rewards will not only be enjoyed for a moment; they are rewards that we will enjoy eternally. We learn from the New Testament that even giving a cool drink of water to someone will bring its reward (Mark 9:41, Matthew 10:42).

We are not talking here about things that are exceedingly difficult to do, nor are they beyond the reach of the normal person. We are talking about just a few words that are spoken in love, or just the simple act of love to benefit other people, and we will receive rewards in heaven for them (1 Corinthians 3:8–15; Psalm 62:12, 19:17; Matthew 5:12, 6:4; Ephesians 6:8; Revelation 2:12).

So being a Christian is collecting eternal rewards from the simple words and acts of love that we offer others in our lives. We can build up treasures in heaven daily. You will hear people say from time to time, "Why do I always have to be the bigger person?" The answer is because you will be greatly rewarded in heaven! The answer is because this is part of helping Jesus usher in the kingdom of God here and now! (Luke 6:35).

Those words and acts of love unleash the power of the kingdom of God to change the hearts and minds of other people so that they too can become loving people. Each spiritually motivated thought, word, and deed motivated by the Holy Spirit brings with it an eternal reward.

The accumulation of material things and great wealth here and now, even having fame and power in this world, can be enjoyable, but they are not what means the most in this world. These are all temporal blessings. These are all things that will be lost when we die.

No one can take these kinds of temporal blessings with them after death. The only things that we can take with us are those things that are born of the Holy Spirit. The only things that we can take with us are the rewards we have earned by doing the will of God in this world. The rewards we receive from words and acts of agape love are more valuable than anything we can gain within this world (Matthew 6:19–21).

If we think about that, that is good news! All the little things that we say and do will not only be rewarding here and now, but they will also be rewards that will be enjoyed for an eternity!

Have you ever done anything for another person and experienced how good you felt because you did it for that person, which made them so happy and made such a big difference in his or her life? Is it not good news to know that the good feeling you feel from doing good to other people will not just be experienced for a few moments here and now but will be experienced and enjoyed for an eternity in heaven?

It is important, however, that we don't get confused and start thinking that these good works save us. No, salvation is by grace through faith in Jesus Christ. We cannot earn our salvation through good works, so no one in heaven can boast that he or she earned his or her way there. No, salvation is a gift of God, received through the grace of God that is found in Christ Jesus. But understand this: those who willingly receive this grace of God unto salvation are empowered by the Holy Spirit to do good works. Those good works will be greatly rewarded in heaven.

With these eternal rewards set before us, do we have anything to look forward to? We sure do! No matter what happens in our lives, we have a bright future ahead of us!

We always have before us more opportunity to gain even greater rewards in the kingdom of heaven. It does not have to be big things; just the little things we say and do that are prompted by God's Holy Spirit will be rewarded and enjoyed eternally. Sharing the truth in love, being kind to those you meet in need, and showing understanding and sympathy are all acts of love done in spirit and in truth that bring eternal rewards.

One note of caution is needed here. People can imitate true acts of love. Those who do are spiritual wolves in sheep's clothing. God only rewards that which is spiritually motivated by the agape love of God. Our love for another must be spiritually real. Saying what people who love another say and doing what people who love others do does not make what you say and do an act of love. Ushering in the kingdom of God is a spiritual endeavor.

Jesus said, "Be careful not to practice your righteousness in front of others to be seen by them. If you do, you will have no reward from your Father in heaven. So, when you give to the needy, do not announce it with trumpets, as the hypocrites do in the synagogues and on the streets, to be honored by others. Truly I tell you, they have received their reward in full" (Matthew 6:1–2).

Like all other aspects of Christian faith and life, it must be a spiritual reality. If you do your works before people with the motivation to gain praise and honor from them, that is the only reward you will get.

God cannot and will not be fooled by those who try to disguise their true motives. God searches the hearts and minds of people and will reward each person accordingly.

Love God and love your neighbor as yourself in spirit and in truth, and your reward in heaven will be great! By sharing the same unconditional love with others that God has shown us in Christ Jesus, we are ushering in the spiritual kingdom of God, and our heavenly Father will reward us for this work of love. This is the ultimately satisfying and eternally rewarding life.

FOURTEEN

Good News! Jesus Is Coming Again!

FAITH KEY #14

A NEW HEAVEN AND EARTH ARE COMING!

> But in keeping with his promise we are looking forward
> to a new heaven and a new earth, where righteousness
> dwells. (2 Peter 3:13)

This world and the life we are experiencing here will come to an end. This is true on a personal level and is true for the whole world as well.

Typically, when we hear the words "The end is near!" it is being spoken by someone who is trying to instill fear in the hearts of people. He or she is trying to give a message of gloom and doom. But for all who trust in the love and mercy of God shown us in Christ Jesus, who embrace the hope of eternal life, the future holds absolutely nothing that we should fear.

The Bible teaches us that there will be a new heaven and a new earth! (Revelation 21:1, Mark 13:31, 2 Peter 3:13). This is not something to fear; this is good news that we should rejoice over and look forward to. This new heaven and earth will be populated with every person who has embraced the Truth and opened their hearts to the mercy and grace of God shown us through Christ Jesus (2 Peter 3:13).

Scripture reveals that in this new creation there will no longer be any tears because everyone will be willingly doing the will of God, and therefore each will be a blessing to others. This new world will comprise those people who willingly allowed their hearts to be filled with the spiritual desires of God.

When we are there, we will all still have our unique human characteristics because, as Jesus taught, we will experience a bodily resurrection (Isaiah 26:19, Daniel 12:2, Job 19:26, Acts 4:2, 1 Corinthians 15:42). We will know those who we have known before. We will meet again those friends and family members who have passed before us that have also looked to God for mercy.

Complete harmony and peace will exist in the new world. We are even told that the wolf will live with the lamb, the calf will lie down with the lion (Isaiah 11:6). There will be complete peace and harmony within nature as well. This means there will no longer be any destructive storms; the weather will always be a blessing for us to enjoy.

Everything will be made new. Anything that we have physically wrong with us today will be completely healed. Those that are blind will see perfectly with 20/20 vision! Those who have been crippled will be completely healed and will enjoy perfect physical health. There will be no sickness or disease. Our new DNA will be a perfected version of our old DNA, and we will live eternally! This will be heaven—our eternal paradise.

No longer will there be a struggle with the desires of the flesh to do the will of God. We will all know the will of God and enthusiastically do the will of God.

The pure agape love of God will fill our hearts. This spiritual love will create within our communities a communion with God and with one another that will generate pure joy and everlasting peace and harmony! Our relationships with other people will only result in the fruits of the spirit being enjoyed by everyone. There will be no injustices. Everyone will do what is right and good in the eyes of the Lord and thereby will be a spiritual blessing to everyone they meet.

What lies before us is paradise! Our struggle here to be happy and to live in peace and harmony with one another will end. This is not something to fear, but something to look forward to with eager anticipation and joy.

There has always been, and there will always be, disagreements about the proper interpretations of the biblical prophesies about the end-times. There are likewise differing views about the timeline of events that will happen before the end of the world.

Thousands of books have been written and hundreds of movies have been made sensationalizing what that experience will be like. While these views and interpretations of the end-times can be entertaining, they add little to what is important—knowing who we are called to be and what we are called to do as the spiritual children of God!

Scripture is abundantly clear that Christ Jesus will come again, and when He does, God's purpose and plan for this world will be completed! (John 14:3; Acts 1:11; Matthew 24:10, 44; Matthew 25). We do not, and we will not, know the day and hour of His return, nor will we need to. God always reveals what is necessary to live as faithful spiritual children of God.

All the signs of His imminent return will be in place (Matthew 24). People will be routinely living their lives as they always do, without a clue about what is about to happen, and suddenly, in the twinkling of an eye, everyone will see Jesus appear in the sky, returning with power and great glory!

In that split second, all who died in Christ Jesus will be raised from the dead (1 Thessalonians 4:13–18, 1 Corinthians 6:14, Isaiah 26:19), and their bodies will be transformed into the imperishable body like that body that Jesus was raised from the dead with (1 Corinthians 15:42, Philippians 3:21, Romans 8:11). Those believers that are still alive will be caught up together in the clouds with those who are raised from the dead, and we will be with Jesus forever (1 Thessalonians 4:17–18).

The return of Christ and the impending end of the world are reasons to rejoice and a reality to find comfort in! It brings with it the eternal life promised in Christ Jesus that will be a life greater than we can even imagine. Living a life where everything people desire, think, say, and do is motivated by love will be a truly blessed life!

The fear associated with the end of our lives and the ultimate end of the world comes from the fact that the "Day of Judgment" comes with the return of Christ. The justice of God demands that each person will reap what they have sown. Each person who has ever lived will be judged on that day according to what he or she has said, done, and not done (Romans 2:6, Matthew 25:1–46).

The spiritual freedom to make our own decisions in life is real, and our responsibility for the decisions we make is also real. Those who refuse to allow the spiritual love of God to govern the desires of their heart will perish. Those who open their hearts to the spiritual love of God shown us in Christ Jesus, and thereby those who share this unconditional love with others, will be greatly rewarded for their acts of love come judgment day.

Let there be no doubt that it matters what we think, say, and do in our lives. We have been saved from our broken spiritual condition and given the Holy Spirit by grace through faith to equip us to live as the spiritual children of God here and now. Those who resist being controlled by self-centered desires and instead share words and deeds of God's unconditional love will be greatly rewarded in the eternal kingdom of God (Matthew 25:14–30). Those who refuse to open their hearts to the love of God and refuse to share this unconditional love with others will be destroyed by God eternally.

FIFTEEN

God Is Trying to Tell You Something!

FAITH KEY #15

YOU WILL EXPERIENCE THE BLESSINGS OF GOD
THROUGH THE RENEWING OF YOUR MIND!

Do not conform to the pattern of this world but be transformed by the renewing of your mind. Then you will be able to test and approve what God's will is his good, pleasing, and perfect will. (Romans 12:2)

If God has given you spiritual "eyes to see and ears to hear" (Isaiah 32:3, Matthew 13:16), and God has been speaking to you through the pages of this book, keep listening! God is trying to tell you so much more! God is trying to tell you something right now to help you grow as one of His spiritual children.

We can see and experience the blessings that come through embracing the truths of Christian faith. I am just one of many witnesses to the truth that God rewards those who seek him. Millions of people have discovered the Truth:

Those who seek God will find Him. (Proverbs 8:17, Hebrews 11:6)

Those who say within their hearts daily, "Speak to me," will be guided by God daily to renew their minds with the Truth, and they will experience the spiritual blessings that come from trusting these truths.

God is continually present and trying to say something to you every day. The spiritual eyes to see and the ears to hear are a gift of God to all who will seek Him in spirit and in truth. God longs for us to experience all the spiritual blessings He has revealed to us through Christ Jesus. Every physical and spiritual need we have is being met by God and can be experienced through active faith in the salvation Jesus has provided through His life, death, and resurrection.

My prayer for you is that the God-given spiritual desire to know the Truth will burn within your heart. I hope that you will look to God daily to reveal to you the Way, the Truth, and the Life of love revealed to us in Christ Jesus. I hope that you will step out in faith believing God is more than willing and able to reveal the truth to you. I believe those who do will experience that He will be and do all that He has promised.

The key to unlocking all the mysteries of life and experiencing the power of God flowing in and through your life is through trusting these fifteen foundational beliefs of Christian faith. Actively trusting and renewing our minds to think in harmony with these beliefs will set our souls free of every fear that confronts us in this life!

The loving presence and power of God is all around us and within us and can be seen and experienced through every detail of His creation. The light that rises every morning, the warmth we need to live, and every breath we take is experiencing the presence, the power, and the love of God.

God has created each of us to be uniquely like Him spiritually, capable of becoming His spiritual children in this world and a living blessing to others.

No one has reason to boast spiritually. We have all tried to live for a time without God. All have turned away spiritually from God and tried living self-centered lives. All have sinned and all thereby have contributed to the pain and suffering in this world.

The law of God does protect us from our spiritual brokenness; like a light in the darkness, it helps us to see what we should be and do. But in the end, it still leaves us facing death, the consequence of our sin, and only reveals to us our helplessness to reunite with God spiritually.

All who will embrace this Truth can likewise discover the unconditional love and mercy God has for us. Because of His love for us, God Himself came to earth in the person of Jesus, to reveal the depth of His love for us, to save us from our spiritual predicament, to suffer the consequences of our sin for us, and pave a spiritual path to eternal life with Him.

All who embrace the Truth of this spiritual love and mercy of God will experience His forgiveness of their sins. They will experience a spiritual rebirth that puts us in a new spiritual union with God. They will become a part of the new creation that God created this existence on earth to produce.

As spiritual children of God, through simple childlike faith, we will receive the gift of the Holy Spirit from our heavenly Father. The Holy Spirit will live in us and teach us how to grow as a spiritual child of God. He will empower us to increasingly become a spiritual blessing in this world and reveal through our acts and words of unconditional love the reality of the spiritual kingdom of God.

Those who share with Jesus the sufferings that come from sharing this Good News with love will be greeted by Christ Jesus at His return with "well done, my good and faithful servant," and will be rewarded with their portion of the inheritance of God in the kingdom of heaven!

God is trying to tell you something right now! Open your heart to the salvation Jesus has provided us and receive the Holy Spirit into your heart, and He will teach you all things! Receive and share this unconditional love of God with others, and you will be greatly rewarded in this world and the coming eternal kingdom of heaven!

God is trying to tell you something right now! If you will listen, you will hear Him!

Amen! "It is so, so let it be!"

PERSONAL NOTE FROM MARK VEE...

I appreciate those who have taken the time to read this book. My goal was to give you an overview of the key Christian views about life that have the power to transform your understanding of the purpose of your life.

To live a life of Christian faith and experience the presence and blessing of God in and through your life, we need to renew our minds, so that our thoughts are in harmony with these biblical truths. Unfortunately, that is not as simple as just flicking a light switch on. There is an ongoing spiritual war for control of our hearts and minds, and what we actively trust to be true.

There have been many things that have happened over the course of my life that have challenged my beliefs that these beliefs are true. During those times, when I am prone to doubt, I go back to square one and ask myself, "What do I really belief is true?" Do I really believe there is a God? Do I really believe He is good? Do I really believe He is love? What do I really believe is God's purpose for life? I go right down the line of these 15 key Christian beliefs, re-establish a clear vision of what I really believe, and thereby, I experience the presence and blessing of God in and through my life anew. I believe the reason this works is because these beliefs are true. I believe if you truly seek God, He will reveal Himself to you and reveal the truth about life to you as well.

I am building an online community of people who desire to increasingly experience the presence and blessings of God in their life and desire to increasingly become a spiritual blessing of God's unconditional love. My online ministry is especially designed to meet the spiritual needs of people who do not regularly attend a local church.

- To learn more about my online Christian ministries, visit me at http://www.markvee.com.
- As an author I am very interested in who reads my books and what comments or questions you may have after reading this book. Please share them with me at http://www.markvee.com/CYBI
- If you found spiritual value in this book and would like to recommend it to others, a "Review" on Amazon will greatly increase the visibility of this book online.

Mark Vee
"Becoming Spiritual Blessings Together…"
http://markvee.com